WHAT WOULD
MACHIAVELLI
DO?

WHAT WOULD MACHIAVELLI DO?

THE ENDS
JUSTIFY
THE MEANNESS

STANLEY BING

HarperBusiness
A Division of HarperCollins*Publishers*

HarperCollins books may be purchased for educational, business, or sales promotional use. For information please write: Special Markets Department, HarperCollins Publishers Inc., 10 East 53rd Street, New York, NY 10022.

FIRST EDITION

Designed by Lindgren/Fuller Design

Printed on acid-free paper

ISBN 0-06-662011-2

00 01 02 03 04 ❖/RRD 10 9 8 7 6 5 4 3 2 1

DEDICATION

In the spirit of the master, I'm going to suppress the impulse to dedicate this book to my family, my friends, my bosses, the people who have influenced my thoughts and shaped my path as I make my way toward its completion. Instead, I'm going to do what Machiavelli would tell me to do, and dedicate this book to myself.

CONTENTS

What Would Machiavelli Do?

ACKNOWLEDGMENTS

I'd like to thank Leonard, my first boss, who kept me waiting in his anteroom for three hours one Friday night in 1982 until I realized that he had left by a separate exit without having the courtesy to tell me he was doing so. He is now a multi-billionaire who works about six hours a week. I'd like to thank Carl, my next boss, for scaring me badly in unimportant business meetings. He is now the biggest landowner in the state of Wyoming, worth more than the gross national product of France. I'd like to thank Dick, who accepted a timely retirement package and left all of us to fend for ourselves after that merger in the early 90s. Most of us didn't make it. But he did, and I'm happy for him. I'd like to thank the Business pages of the *New York Times*, for keeping the abuse of power always in vogue by unfailingly extolling the virtues of the gigantic Machiavellian monsters that shape our working environment in every industry on a daily basis. I'd also like to thank my current bosses, from whom I've learned a lot, but only in a very good way. Hi, guys!

On the other hand, I'm not going to thank my friends and editors at *Fortune*, because frankly, they're too nice. Lord knows how they've made it this far. The same goes for my friend and editor at Harper-Collins, David Hirshey, who tries to follow the precepts of this book and most often fails.

I'd also like to acknowledge the enormous contribution of my wife and kids to the general framework of my personal and professional life, but what kind of mean guy would do a thing like that?

PREFACE

How in the world did that person get to where he is today?" You hear that question everywhere lately, as people stare at the cover of *Fortune* or *Business Week* or the pen-and-ink drawings in the *Wall Street Journal* and contemplate the great and powerful leader of the moment who just made his second hundred million or, more likely than not, his fourth billion.

"How can I be more like that person, in the sense that I rule everything that comes near me and enjoy compensation by the ton?" you hear people ask not only themselves, but each other.

And it's a darn good question. Are the super-powerful giants who mold our lives different than you or me? Of course they are. Well, at least they're different than you. Because you don't yet walk in the path of the truly successful, those who are guided by the basic teaching of the simple bureaucrat from Florence who spoke to us five hundred years ago or thereabouts.

Throughout our time here on earth, we all have a choice. To do things the mediocre way . . . or Machiavelli's way.

Some choose to follow the easy road. They allow their

human impulses to guide them. They try to be decent. They view other people as free individuals who have a right to live their own lives. They are embarrassed by power and greed and manipulation. In short, they find their own little cubbyhole and crawl into it. These are the men and women whom you see on the train or bus or subway every morning in their humdrum designer knockoffs, eating a dry little muffin from a brown paper bag and reading, confused and dejected, about the next Internet millionaire. In other words, you or me. Or at least you. I very often drive to work in my company car.

And then there are the other people. They rise like gas bubbles in Moët to the top of any corporate hierarchy. They make decisions. They make money. They make other people do what they want. They rule. Because they are the people who every day, in every way, ask themselves the key question that transforms a middle manager into a CEO: "What would Machiavelli do?"

This book attempts to answer that question for all aspects of your life, because obviously, you need help.

When the world calls upon you to be mean, you're nice.

When the world requires you to be lousy, you remain decent.

When the world needs you to be decisive, even though you don't really know what to do . . . you ask other people for their opinions. Sometimes you even pay a consultant, you fool.

On most weekends, you like to spend time with your family and friends, and assume that others would like to do the same.

You're sometimes satisfied with what you have.

You want to be happy, and to make other people happy if you can.

In other words, you're doomed. Doomed to the middle. Doomed to be one of those who are acted upon, not one of those who act. That's all right. We can take care of that.

This book will take you by the shoulders, shake you, and make you begin to live your sorry life differently. To take stock of a situation and ask yourself, before you act: *What would Machiavelli do?*

And the answer, in almost all cases, is: *Whatever is necessary.*

That's right. Machiavelli would advise you to do *whatever is necessary*, and that's it. The goal? To grow your personal power. Remember it. Live by it. Because your personal power and nobody else's *is* the ultimate good. For society. For the world in which we live. For puppies and kittens and all the little children.

Simple? Sure. But not so simple that you don't need this book. Put it in your briefcase. Take it on your train. Sneak it into meetings in one of those cheap fake-leather binders they give you because they think you're too stupid to bring your own pen and paper. And when Mr. Roover leans over and begins to work on you about the

upcoming budget, or the fourth-quarter numbers, or the productivity of your department, or the future of the industry as he sees it and where he expects you to play a role in it—*stop!*

Lean back. Ask yourself: What would Machiavelli do? And if you don't know, don't worry. You have this book.

Unless you're standing up at some bookstore right now, trying to decide whether to buy it and rifling through its contents without paying for it. If that's you, close the book right now, you pathetic loser. Go to the cash register immediately, pay for at least one copy, if not two. Go home. Read it cover to cover. It won't take long. I didn't want it to be too weighty or demanding, because I know you have no real attention span, particularly since you started cruising the Net every night instead of reading cheesy magazines and mail-order catalogs the way you used to. For that reason, I also chopped up the advice in here into digestible little nuggets, because I know that's the way you like things. I made the whole book easy to read, easy to understand, almost impossible not to buy for people who are ambitious, smart, and insecure. Hopefully by now I've created the fear in you that if you do not listen to me, you will fail. Maybe not today, not this week, but soon, and for the rest of your life. And operating under that fear, you will do what I want you to do.

Good!

Let's get mean.

INTRODUCTION

Not long ago I was approached by a young manager by the name of Bob who was having a problem managing a subordinate.

The workload was quite heavy in their department, and as Friday was approaching it was clear that the required duties might very well stretch into the weekend. Sadly, Bob's deputy, Mary, was scheduled to go on a long-planned vacation that very Saturday. If Mary were to go, life would become very difficult for Bob, who had an important golf game he'd been looking forward to since his last golf game the prior weekend.

"I don't know," said Bob. "I'm under an incredible amount of stress. If I don't get in eighteen, I may not be able to handle the pressure next week. But I feel bad for Mary."

Bob's boss, Ned, who had long ago earned his first Mercedes—and not a baby 350 either, but one of those big 500s that eat up more than one entire lane as they burn asphalt at 75 mph—swiftly and rather bluntly inquired: "Bob, let me help you out. Answer this question. If Machiavelli were here, what would he do?"

Bob thought about it for a moment, then, his worry lines returning to their usual flabbiness, shot back: "He would pretend to have forgotten about Mary's vacation altogether, put an enormous amount of work on her shoulders at the last minute, and wait to see if she had the guts to take off under those conditions. Of course, she probably wouldn't."

Sure enough, things worked out perfectly—Mary rescheduled her vacation, Bob got in his round of golf (although he was annoyed several times by cellular phone calls while on the course) and Bob's boss was happy because all the work got done while he was in Gstaad, skiing!

Amazing how if you want the right answer, all you have to do is ask the right question.

This funny story illuminates the basic precepts we're going to be employing: People in the workplace who wish to succeed, have fun, and always get things their way should be intimately aware of what Machiavelli, the first truly modern, amoral thinker, would have to say on any subject that might come to pass during the normal course of business.

Nobody can really understand Machiavelli's actual writing today, however, because it is too literate, too grounded in meaningless social, political, and military anecdote, to remain interesting to anyone with normal intelligence, attention span, and patience.

Lacking an ability to read Machiavelli, people like

you are going to need books like this one to explain how his teaching can help you become very big, very powerful, and very rich. Some are written by intelligent people who are interested in Machiavelli. This is not one of them. You're not interested in Machiavelli. You're interested in yourself. Why waste your time on anything else?

This book boils down the path of the master into an overall strategy with the absolute minimum of sentiment, and the greatest amount of selfishness and brutality. In so doing, we create a way of operating that anyone sufficiently nasty can embrace with great creativity. Best of all, once you get used to the Machiavellian way, you will find it liberating, honest, and fun!

The basis of Machiavellian leadership is to keep in mind that *Machiavelli guides our every action*. Put another way, Machiavelli's thinking is user-friendly in every situation, be it social, professional, or somewhere in-between.

A Few Words About the Master

Niccolo Machiavelli was born in Italy during the Renaissance, which took place, for the most part, four or five hundred years ago. The circumstances of his birth were relatively humble, but I don't know that much about them. That's not my job. I'm here to look

at the big picture, to give you the executive summary. If you want to know more specific stuff, look it up. That's your job. I must warn you, there may be a test on this material in the middle of a meeting in which you could be publicly humiliated, so I'd suggest you get busy.

At any rate, our prophet and master was a mid-level bureaucrat who for the best part of his career worked for a variety of departments reporting in to the Prince of Florence. He did a lot of traveling and spent a considerable amount of time representing the corporation on the road. This was when Florence was still a freestanding entity, before it was acquired and merged into Italy. So Machiavelli and his entire culture pretty much considered their enterprise to be the be-all and end-all as a global power on a path toward double-digit growth.

The biggest corporate officer of all was Lorenzo de Medici. Smart, brutal, and not a nice guy except when he felt like it, Mr. Medici and his court were very political, and at some point Machiavelli got on the wrong side of his boss. It's not important why. Who cares? It's not any more germane than the reason why Sumner Redstone suddenly decided a few years ago that he had to be rid of Frank Biondi, who to all intents and purposes looked to be an excellent number two and successor at Viacom. He just did, that's all. And that's what counts.

Machiavelli backed the wrong joint venture, or something like that. Things being what they were at that stage of the game, young Niccolo wasn't just sent to a depressing field office in Skokie to work with the Quality Assurance team. He was remanded to prison, where he sat around thinking of ways to get himself back to the thirty-fifth floor. On the bright side, he wasn't killed, the way he might have been if he reported to a different Italian family several hundred years later.

Sitting and thinking, thinking and sitting, Machiavelli, like so many prophets before him, was purified during his time in the wilderness. And since he was a very good writer, he wrote.

What emerged from the white heat of his imagination, parched from his long stint in the career desert, was a brief, timely letter of advice to his prince on how to become the ultimate senior manager. Medici liked what he read, exercised a full measure of executive amnesia, and Machiavelli, robed in a bright and shining success, was welcomed back to a nice corner office with full honors. His fame has only grown in the years since.

The master has been gone from our presence for quite some time now. But his teaching has remained with us, and is now the core strategy by which the few, generally quite short people have come to lead the rest of the human race to a variety of ends. For

the most part, these individuals are fine to work for (and with) as long as they get their way. But getting their way is what their lives are all about—and these people are focused, man.

And for them there is but one message from which the entire fount of wisdom springs:

The ends justify the meanness.

Don't like it? Get over it, you sniveling tree hugger. That's the way things are. If you haven't got the stomach for true success, that's all right. Go be a folk singer or a graphic designer or a social worker or some damn thing like that. The world has need for people like you as well.

But if you're serious about the path to enlightenment and lucrative stock options, go quietly with us in the noise and haste as we take a look at our lives and ask the one pertinent question for those who wish to conquer the twenty-first century:

"What would Machiavelli do?"

Answer? He would play to win.

Hurdles in Your Way

There are some. Let's look at them.

OBSTACLE 1: OBSCURITY

As I indicated, the fact that it's very difficult to understand anything the master says sometimes gets in the way of our ability to walk, straight and secure, down his path.

> *Both physical bodies and political bodies are ever in process of transformation, analogous one to the other. Hence it is possible to formulate laws descriptive of processes in each area.*
>
> —MACHIAVELLI, *THE PRINCE*

Huh? And that's lucid compared with the master's discussions of how King Ludovico of Fresnia conquered his adversary, Queen Rhumba of Tasmania. Can you wrap your mind around that kind of stuff?

We do, however, care a lot about examples and anecdotes that speak to what passes for current history today, exactly the kinds of stories that Machiavelli used in his teachings, stories that will probably mean nothing to people five hundred years from now:

⊕ Bill Gates eating up every competitor in his path, using all the leverage provided by his dominance of

operating systems to squeeze smaller players out of business, coming close to world domination of all future technologies when stopped by the government of a nation just slightly larger than his;

- "Chain Saw" Al Dunlap, one of the most brutal and unsentimentally selfish senior managers in the history of twentieth-century capitalism, crying, literally shedding tears, to a reporter from the *Wall Street Journal* after he himself was booted from his position at Sunbeam, a company he had virtually destroyed during his brief time at its helm;

- Howard Hughes, the great industrialist and visionary of his generation, deathly afraid of germs, demanding that all of his fruit cocktail cans be thoroughly wiped off before they were opened by sterilized can openers;

- The most recent president of the United States . . . but let's talk more about him later.

And so many, many others who five hundred years ago would have been wearing lace and silly garters and fighting with swords and daggers. They are our princes. And they play by the rules established by Machiavelli half a millennium ago.

OBSTACLE 2: SENTIMENT

Most people are hamstrung by things like affection for fellow employees, honesty, desire to appear to be a

"nice person," and other crippling limitations not suffered by the truly powerful and successful.

This book will attempt to eradicate those impulses in you, but you're going to have to cooperate.

This will take two things:

1. Courage: The ability to discover the "real" you that is hidden behind centuries of cultivation, to root out that unpleasant toadlike creature within you and give him or her the keys to the car.

2. Practice: Big people didn't get that way overnight. They started out as human beings and then became horrible. You're going to have to put the pedal to the metal every day, no matter how kind, small, soft, or vulnerable you're feeling on any given issue. Don't worry. As you do it more, it will become easier, until you're a really despicable troll without even trying. At that moment, look around and see how well you're doing, financially and professionally. You'll be amazed.

In short, asking ourselves the question *"What would Machiavelli do?"* is a good beginning, but it's only a beginning. We have to live Machiavelli, every day, in all we do, from the moment we send back our toast at breakfast to the last disgruntled remark we make to our miserable partner as our heads hit the

pillow at night. To live true to the vision of the master, we must be as selfish, narcissistic, manipulative, driven, and creative in getting what we want as we can be, not just in our important business actions, but where it really counts: in our hearts.

You can do it. This book will help.

OBSTACLE 3: OTHER PEOPLE

For the most part, they're going to hate you.

The hell with them.

Nobody said power was a popularity contest. In fact, it's the opposite of a popularity contest. Most of the time, it's an unpopularity contest.

Some people will love you, though.

The people you bring along with you to the top—the ones who do what you want, fast, efficient, with no tearful burbling, who are willing to lay down their lives for you—they're likely to love you, because they've given themselves to you and would feel really bad about themselves if they didn't like you at least a little. That's the thing about smaller people. They need to invest their masters with human qualities, even if you don't have any. Look at the good press Slobodan Milosevic got in all the hot Serbian media. They thought he was terrific. Until he lost.

People you pay a lot of money will also like you, particularly if you give them cars.

And like I said, the hell with them if they don't like you. A $50 cigar and a bottle of single-malt scotch can be awesome company after a long day crushing people.

It's Never Too Late

I started in business in 1981. I was a pretty good person. Not a great person, maybe, but as good as most. Now, almost twenty years later, I'm a lot more successful, and if I keep going the way I am, by the time I'm, say, sixty? I'll be a real dick, and very successful, too.

There's no reason you can't make the same kind of strides. Of course it comes easier to some than to others. People born in the 1960s seem capable of crass selfishness and overweening ambition that puts the older baby boomers to shame. But we of the over-the-counterculture bow to no one in our obnoxious belief that we were born to impose our wishes and worldview on others. And we're healthier and sharper than any generation our age in the history of the world. We're going to be around for a while, and there's no reason we can't run things right. That is, for us.

Obviously, those who wish to fight the great bulge of plump, neurotic, pushy boomers, cut a swath through our increasingly soft underbelly, and make some serious dough by the time they're thirty, or even forty, are well advised to take up their Machiavelli, too.

Not only CEOs can behave like princes. Lying. Manipulation. Displays of false anger. Displays of real anger. Threats. Blandishments. Cruelty. Gross abuse of loyalty. Guilt production in people who misperceive the senior officer as a father or mother figure—all these tactics and more represent the kind of thinking that should be made available to all levels of management, not just the big guys.

You can use them, too, if you've got the brains, the guts, and the stamina. And you ask the right question, the big one, the alpha and omega of the power we seek:

What would Machiavelli do?

Let's find out.

What Would Machiavelli Do?
✗ ✗ ✗

He would exploit himself only slightly less than he exploits others

I think while I nap,
so it's not a waste of time.
—MARTHA STEWART

These guys get up at the break of day. But they don't really have to *get up*, because they don't sleep. And they don't sleep because they *can't*. There's a famous story about IBM chieftain Lou Gerstner, a notorious behemoth, who reportedly turned to his wife one fine Sunday afternoon and said, "I really can't wait to get to the office tomorrow." Most guys are sitting around waiting for the barbecue to heat up, a nice frosty tumbler of Absolut resting on their midsection. Not Lou Gerstner. He can't wait to get to the office.

That's a powerful asset.

Si Newhouse, the lil' Mini-Me who has marched Condé Nast into the twenty-first century, often ends his workday at, like, three or four in the afternoon. This is not because he's laid-back. It's because he's

1

tired after a twelve-hour day. That's right. He starts out at three or four in the morning. What work can you get done at that hour? Thinking, ladies and gentlemen. It's called thinking.

As I write this, I'm heading off to meet with a grand dragon of industry who keeps exactly those amazing hours. He's up at four. In by five. Answers his own phone until eight or so. What level of activity do you think he requires of his people?

Can this kind of insane kind of sleep-disturbance be taught? I don't know. But it's never too early to start.

I was once hanging out with a young prince who was even then shaping the *weltanschauung* of a $3-billion corporation. I knew he did very little, when you got right down to it. His role was basically to lurk about until the chairman decided it was time to do something. He would then be called in to kill it. This didn't take much of an effort. But he was one of those guys who believed it was important to be at the ready. Readiness was all. Be prepared. For him, being there was 99 percent of the gig. So he was there. Big fucking deal, right? When you start making 500K a year you can criticize the strategy.

So I said to him: "Gee, Roger, the sunrise must be very beautiful from up here." I thought I was kidding. "Yes," he says. "It is." This kind of throws me, because a normal human being, like a dog, tries to sleep as much as possible. But these guys are not dogs.

They eat dogs.

What Would Machiavelli Do?
✗ ✗ ✗

He would be unpredictable, and thus gain the advantage

> *I didn't want to harm the man. I thought he was a very nice gentleman. Soft-spoken. I thought so right up to the moment I cut his throat.*
> —MURDERER PERRY SMITH, QUOTED BY
> TRUMAN CAPOTE IN *IN COLD BLOOD*

Impulsiveness. Volatility. Capriciousness. Changeability. In short, nobody knows what you're likely to do next. Whatever you do, though, they know it's going to be big. Big and potentially very, very bad. Also good. Don't you just love that look on their faces? Aren't they cute when they can't figure out which direction that blow is going to come from?

This quality of rampaging unpredictability is a well-known tool used by terrorists, authoritarian brainwashers, and those who wish to command and dominate others. It's used because it works better than straight-out intimidation, which can be anticipated and psychologically prepared for.

The great Machiavellian therefore staggers his or her behavior so those around can never truly prepare a defense against incoming management.

Steve Brill, the renowned editor, publisher, man-about-media and bully, is famous for this kind of on-the-one-hand/on-the-other-hand treatment of organisms beneath him. His people report liking Steve Number One quite a bit as a boss, mentor, and all-around nurturing genius, doling out health club memberships and dinners at fancy restaurants. But, according to staffers, there was just no telling when Steve Number Two would pop out, firing that very same person or scratching little witticisms on writers' copy like, "Have you ever considered suicide?"

The really great princes have a leg up on people like you and me, because we'll have to fake it a little bit. They're doing what comes naturally. They have the benefit of being genuinely inconsistent. Inside, they're not integrated into one coherent character that modulates what they do. They're huge, dynamic, and fragmented—*and they always simply do what they feel like doing*. We'll talk more about that later.

The key is being excessive on both ends. Very nice. Very mean. Big, big swings. Gigantic pleasure. Towering rage. Like being a kid again, isn't it?

I used to work for a guy who was a real mean bastard. No, that's too simple. Sometimes Phil was a true gentleman. He could talk expansively to small and

large alike, and could dispense praise and Olympian destruction with equal largesse. The only question was, which Phil was going to show up? Good Phil was all right. Rational. Courteous. Logical in his demands. Bad Phil had beady little eyes and a fondness for firing and rehiring people on the same day. One time he told a senior vice president, with whom he had been chatting affably just a few moments before, to go sharpen some pencils. As the dazed officer was leaving with a fistful of number twos, Phil screamed after him, "And don't call me Phil!" This was the first time any of us had heard that one. Would we now be demoted to the level of pencil sharpener for calling Phil "Phil"?

I later saw this same victimized individual yelling at his secretary, with whom he normally had a very nice relationship. Phil's management style was permeating the entire organization.

That's leadership.

This is not to advise you to be a mean bastard. That's easy. The goal here is to keep people off their feed by making them read you like a barometer every time they have to face you. This makes everything they do feel like it counts.

What Would Machiavelli Do?

✗ ✗ ✗

He would be in love with his destiny

I see myself as an instrument of a will greater than my own and I really try to keep myself connected to that. All my life I have always known I was born to greatness.

—OPRAH WINFREY

Some of us have destinies. Some of us don't. If you don't believe you have one, you don't. Sorry. It's really difficult to manufacture this kind of belief. It's possible that it has to be given to you by your mother.

If you don't believe that you have a destiny yet, you'd better get busy. There are many you can choose. Like:

1. I'm up from the depths. I came out of nowhere. I'm going someplace big, ma!
2. I may be quiet and studious, but underneath it all I'm a killer destined to dominate others with the speed and power of my intellect.
3. God has selected me for important work. His will be done.
4. Of all the most evil things that walk this world, I

am the worst, and am destined to be their ruler.
5. I'm gonna be a big rock 'n' roll star.

They're not too complicated. In fact, a good destiny is always simple to the point of stupidity. The good news is that there are as many destinies as there are people who need them.

To create an entire belief system built on this incredibly thin platform, you're going to need to start deluding yourself. A lot of guys are way ahead of you, so you'd better hurry up.

What Would Machiavelli Do?
✗ ✗ ✗

He would be, for the most part, a paranoid freak

I attribute Intel's ability to sustain success to being constantly on the alert for threats, either technological or competitive in nature. The word paranoia *is meant to suggest that attitude, an attitude that constantly looks over the horizon for threats to your success.*
—ANDY GROVE, CHAIRMAN, INTEL

We've already tipped our sterile paper hat to Howard Hughes, who was so paranoid that he surrounded himself with well-scrubbed men willing to wipe off his spoons and doorknobs to protect him from swarms of bacilli.

How foolish he was. He didn't have to be so afraid of germs. It was the people around him he should have kept a better eye on. They eventually destroyed him. It wasn't the paranoia that was the mistake. It was its target.

That's what Machiavelli would do. He would always be paranoid. But he would be paranoid about the right

8

things. Cheerfully. Proactively. But paranoid? Always.

There are people who view paranoia as a disease of some sort. You often hear it referred to as a mental illness, and certainly in the world at large it seems to have a downside. In business, however, managed paranoia is the only serious strategy.

It is, however, a very serious strategy indeed. In the wrong hands, it can be devastating. Richard Nixon, for example, spent a fair amount of his workday assembling enemies lists made up of people who really and truly *did* hate him. Did that make him crazy? I think not. In the end, however, Nixon didn't drive his paranoia. He let it drive him. And it helped to bring about his spectacular, entertaining downfall.

It doesn't always happen that way, at least not quite so fast. There's no reason you can't make a high level of quite sensible paranoia work for you.

In fact, a strong paranoid stance can be the best possible positioning for a successful stint at the top of any corporate enterprise. Why shouldn't you assume that everyone is against you? It's more rational than believing that they're on your side.

A creative, sane paranoid posture is made up of the following components:

⊕ Mistrust of others: Sure, they've been your friends and supporters so far. That doesn't mean you don't need to watch them very, very carefully.

- ⊕ Hatred of the enemy: There are so many of them. They want you dead. You must kill them first.
- ⊕ Obsessive organization of reality to meet your needs: The real world is unbearably threatening. Shape the one around you so that it bears very little resemblance to the real thing. You can do this by surrounding yourself with sycophants, delegating all nonessential activity to them, conducting your life in a hermetically sealed succession of environments—offices, boardrooms, hotels, bars, restaurants, limousines, and town cars—that maintain your bubble, and never receive unmanaged news. This involves the employment of "tasters" who can take the bite out of reality by sampling what you hear, read, who you see, what you think about, before it gets to you.

This should give you plenty of time to sit around stewing about stuff. That's what Machiavelli would do. You'll also need:

- ⊕ A henchman (or woman): Your paranoid style probably comes with an attendant unwillingness to get too close to people. They make noise, resist your will, and generally have germs, sometimes a lot of germs. Also, people want to shake hands all the time. Some of their hands are fine. Others are

not. They can also get into your face about something of no importance whatsoever and derail your mind for hours afterward. When it comes to other people . . . who needs 'em? A good surrogate is an integral part of your effort to wipe out reality.

◈ A killer's heart: If you find things that don't comfortably fit into your happy worldview, you've got to be willing to stamp them out with prejudice. Just zap them. You'll be glad you did. We'll talk about a couple of techniques later.

◈ Some kind of medicine: Even the sanest paranoid in the world needs something to take the edge off now and then. People in show business, sports, and investment banking tried cocaine for a while, but it was bad for them and only heightened their paranoia. Xanax and Prozac work well, but may inhibit certain Machiavellian drives. Try very cold Bombay Sapphire martinis, straight up with a few big, plump olives in them, which seem to provide a healthful tonic any paranoid can live with on a daily basis.

And for goodness sake, don't forget to leave at least 90 percent of your paranoia at the office! It's a great way to manage your professional life, but as a personal strategy, it stinks!

What Would Machiavelli Do?
✗ ✗ ✗

He would always be at war

At IBM Gerstner flashed a large photograph of Microsoft Corp. chairman Bill Gates on a screen.
"This man wakes up hating you," he snapped to managers. The message: You've got to hate him back.

—COMPUTER RESELLER NEWS

Good for Lou Gerstner! He's a meanie, and his competitors know it.

You know, friends, all that paranoia can be exhausting if you don't spend at least a little time actually kicking somebody's ass now and then. Here's how to do it.

⊕ Show the flag! Use your logo: Put it on stuff and give it to all your people. Shirts. Pins. Watches. Fanny packs. If folks don't get a little misty when they see your logo, you're not doing your job, bubba. On a more local level, if that's necessary, they should feel that way about your department. If that's no good either, perhaps they feel good about your floor. Your corner of the floor. No? How do they feel about you? Maybe you'd better

postpone this war while you go out and find an army.

- Identify the enemy: It's easy. Who's pissing you off? Why should they be permitted to live?

- Choose the time! I find the best time to attack people is very early in the morning, when they don't know where the incoming is going to come in from yet, or at the end of the afternoon, when they think the worst is behind them.

- Pick your terrain! Location! Location, location, location. You can't fight a war without knowing about location. On the phone is as good a place as any. Also, behind the other guy's back is a very good location, too. I hate fighting people face-to-face, don't you?

- Assemble the troops! Sound the trumpet! Then it's your job to sit around, or stand and pace, while planning, plotting, and fuming, and of course doing a little other business and personal stuff. You are the white-hot energy center! Give the rest of the wartime duties to good lieutenants, who are a lot more trustworthy, humane, and courageous than you are, and probably manage large groups of people better than you do.

- Discipline! Loose organizational structures, where people have no idea who they're reporting to and where their ultimate allegiance lies, tend to fray in times of conflict. Control flows downhill. Keep

the sphincters of those around you tight and the whole organization will march in lockstep.

- ⊕ Target the money: What's bad for us is bad for business and that could mean a) no budget money to spend on the things we wanna do; b) no job for some of us, maybe, if this kind of thing continues; c) no bonus, for those of you that get them; d) no value to those stock options we gave to all employees last year instead of a long-term pension plan.
- ⊕ Fight! Fight! Fight! Get together with yourself at the end of the day. Did you win? Did you draw? Do you want to fight the same guy tomorrow? No? Then the war is over!
- ⊕ Do it all over again! Still fighting yesterday's battle? Good luck. If not, honestly, isn't there at least one son-of-a-bitch out there who's really asking for it?

Skillful use of paranoia paired with a generally warlike stance is the bedrock upon which all Machiavellian rulership is based.

Business is more complicated than true warfare because you can't really kill people, which would make things a whole lot easier. When you've won a battle in business, you often have to merge with the conquered party, interact with them, or ask them for their support on the Borzoi Project.

The continuous wartime footing approach is espe-

cially useful for managers who cannot establish genuine affection and mutual regard within their organizations without it. Blood lust aimed outward is more effective than the same emotion focused internally—at you.

Now get out there and kill . . . whoever!

What Would Machiavelli Do?
✗ ✗ ✗

He would cultivate a few, well-loved enemies

*It's impossible to get to the level
I want to without making a lot of enemies.*
—SCOTT RUDIN, FILM PRODUCER

Scott Rudin is in the entertainment business, a spectacularly vicious and underhanded profession where people triumph not only over the downfall of their enemies, but rejoice likewise in the failure of their friends.

In fact, out in LA it's sometimes tough to tell the difference. You play golf with both, laughing like maniacs the whole time. You see both at the same restaurants every day, at the same tables. You talk on the phone every day with both. You sit on industry panels with both. When you see either, you put your arms around them and kiss them smartly on the cheek. . . .

Come to think of it, maybe it's easier than we thought. You don't do any of those things with your friends.

Rudin adds, "This is a town where people don't root for you unless they know you're dying—and they've seen the lab reports."

Not long ago the president of a major broadcasting network, a guy I'll call Chet, was (and remains, as far as I know) a very smart and able guy, very attractive and likable, if suffering from the ubiquitous shortness issue that seems to beset so many senior officers in this world.

Anyhow, network television being the psychotically competitive enterprise it is, eventually every leader, no matter how able, driven, or Machiavellian, bites the dust. And so one day a bell at corporate headquarters in New York tolled for the little prince in LA, and it became known to several close friends of Chet that his very long career at this organization was about to come to an end.

What is interesting about this not unprecedented event was the enormous scramble that went on among his friends to tell good old Chet the bad news once they knew for sure it was about to leak. The thinking was that it would be more humane for Chet to hear it from a friend. So naturally, a lot of friends were falling all over themselves trying to get Chet on the horn.

The brass ring, ironically, went to Butterworth, the equally tiny titan at the head of a rival network. It is said that the news was told with great delicacy and

tact, on a Sunday night, so that Chet would not have to read it in tomorrow's trades. The fact that it was Butterworth who told him the news made people laugh, though. It was rich! And what a coup for Butterworth! Everybody loved it out there.

In such a world, there's a very thin line between your friends and your enemies. But is your world all that different, really? Why not assume the worst? Machiavelli would. And he'd advise a different worldview than other people, too.

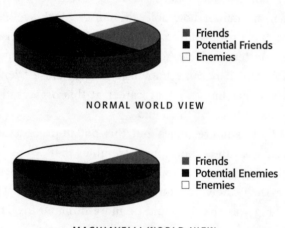

NORMAL WORLD VIEW

■ Friends
■ Potential Friends
☐ Enemies

MACHIAVELLI WORLD VIEW

■ Friends
■ Potential Enemies
☐ Enemies

Don't worry. We're not at war again. You don't need to fight with this enemy. On the contrary, the enemy is there for you, at a distance. Don't be afraid to pull him closer into an actual embrace—or push

him away when it suits you. He's there to measure your success by . . . to illuminate the good things you do with his envy . . . to make you happy when he sucks wind . . . to challenge you when he does well. God bless him!

Yes, a great enemy is to be cherished, nurtured, and loved, just like a friend.

True Machiavellians who are serious about their hatreds as well as their loves, like Mr. Nixon, have a list. Not a long list like his. But a good, solid grouping of the few important enemies whose death, at first a source of rejoicing, would leave a bittersweet hole where your living, breathing enmity used to be.

Here's how to make a list that will stand the test of time:

1. Begin in anger. There are, in a given week, three, four, five people who have enraged you on personal level, right?
2. Nurture your rage, but do not feed it with tinder. You will notice that over the course of the next few days, you will feel more moderate about several of the persons you wanted to have impaled on a spike just last Tuesday. Allow yourself to mellow. If you're very lucky, every now and then, the hate you feel for one of these individuals will not pass, like a stone. It will, to your surprise, have grown. If so, congratulations. You have a candidate.

3. Look at your existing list. Be aware that there is only room for five, at most, on it, unless you are a very big screwball indeed. An overly long list is a burden, and creates problems of its own, leading more than one person to have done stupid, self-destructive things. So take a name off before you put another one on, if you can.

4. Add the new name. Then open a bottle of champagne and have a drink. A new enemy is an event to be savored.

5. Begin plotting and taking active steps to destroy your enemy from a distance, but do nothing to escalate your status to wartime footing. Business wars should not be based on hatred of an enemy, no matter how loathsome he might be. Business wars should be based on strategic necessity, and may, in fact, be conducted against friends as often as the opposite.

Don't hesitate, by the way, to have your enemy over for drinks, meetings, and occasional conversation. The worst thing you can do is get out of touch.

He would have a couple of good friends, too

A good friend is hard to find.
—ANONYMOUS

You've got to have friends.
—BETTE MIDLER

It is, however, only an insane person who doesn't have at least one halfway decent friend. You have a right to one, no matter what kind of monster you may be, or become.

Even Hitler had friends of some sort. Guys that hung around with him, talked a little shop, kicked around solutions to things.

Richard Nixon, one of the most tragically unlikable men ever to enter public life, had Walter Annenberg and Bebe Rebozo to hunker down with when everybody else was against him.

Pals, you know. Don't try to do it without pals.

What Would Machiavelli Do?
✗ ✗ ✗

He would acquire his neighbor

Working on a deal is better than a climax.
—D. K. LUDWIG, LATE BILLIONAIRE,
FOUNDER NATIONAL CONTAINER CORP.

Bang! Zoom!
—RALPH KRAMDEN

I was on the job for fifteen years before I learned what business itself was all about. Or rather, what it's not.

It's not about offering a product or service.

It's not about providing jobs for people.

It's not about running something right, making a difference, winning for the team, taking lunch, brunch, drinks, retreats, or loyalty to Uncle Bob.

It's not about Quality.

It's not about golf.

It's about one thing, and one thing only. Getting bigger.

For big Machiavellis who operate macro-style, this means gobbling up other entities and building cash flow.

You could do everything right, and your core business—whatever it is—would only grow 4 percent a year. And that would be fine for the little fellow, you know? But not for Wall Street. Wall Street wants you to grow 15 percent a year! Who can grow 15 percent a year just on improved quality and stuff like that? Nobody.

No, growth that makes Wall Street pop up and stay there requires you to buy your competitor and put him out of business. The prince who wishes to make the stock dance must *buy revenue*. That is, purchase entire companies whose incoming cash can simply be applied to your own *to give the illusion of enormous revenue growth*, quarter after quarter, year after year.

This insight is driving the beautiful consolidation progress that's now taking place in big oil, telecommunications, transportation, publishing, food, and new and old media. "Come together," wrote John Lennon. And we are! We are!

One day, ladies and gentlemen, and that day is not far from here and now, there will be eight or nine towering, luminous global corporations that are bigger and more powerful than any government this planet has ever seen. Bigger than Rome! Bigger than Byzantium! It's . . . [your company here]!

You can be a part of that. But only if you start eating the other guy, making his operation a part of yours.

On your level, of course, that's a pretty meaningless concept. What's the chance of you eating anything bigger than a sandwich?

It doesn't matter. No matter what's the size of your principality, you've got stuff to acquire. Look around you. Isn't there somebody you could control more? Some small person, who works next to you on the floor, say. Or your boss, who is extremely paranoid and needy? How about him?

Inexorably, like a wheat thresher, move across the field before you, eating as much as you can as you go.

Grow! Take things! Come on! Get going!

What Would Machiavelli Do?
✗ ✗ ✗

He would think BIG

*It is our intention to own areas in communication.
I don't mean to sound egomaniacal, but Perry
Como used to own Christmas on TV. By own
I mean monopolize and influence.*

—MARTHA STEWART EMPLOYEE

It is not, unfortunately, possible to own everything. That doesn't mean you can't try. Cars. Pens. Other people. But you've got to think BIG. Not big . . . BIG.

You've got to want it all.

What is in your sane little mind right now? Double it. Triple it. Expand your goal until it is so bloated, so gigantized, that you barely recognize it.

Like cars? Jerry Seinfeld has twenty or thirty of them. So what if you can only have two? It's the thought that counts.

Like nice houses? Mick Jagger has houses peppered around the world, where they lie gathering dust until he returns with his newest supermodel to live in them for a little while. Why not you?

Unlimited possessions, however, are only the smallest

part of thinking BIG. It's the desire for BIG power that distinguishes the kind of prince/princess you want to be.

Complete the following statements:

1. I would be satisfied with . . . a) a billion dollars; b) a trillion dollars; c) a gazillion dollars; d) I have no idea, but I'm really not satisfied *right now*.

2. If I had a boat, it would be . . . a) a perfect jewel; b) very, very big— huge really; c) the biggest boat in the whole world; d) I have no idea, but it would be bigger than yours.

3. I believe other people . . . a) should do what I want them to do; b) should fall down and kiss my feet; c) should lie down in my path, so I can walk on them; d) There are other people?

4. On vacation, I . . . a) have a lot of fun; b) have more fun than you; c) spend a lot of money; d) bought my largest competitor and spun off a tracking stock.

5. By the end of today, I will . . . a) get home without incident; b) make that big deal! c) get my picture in the *New York Times*; d) Fuck you, asshole.

If you answered d) to all of these questions, move on to the next chapter.

What Would Machiavelli Do?
✗ ✗ ✗

He would move forward like a great shark, eating as he goes

The whole forward momentum thing is such a key part of my nature. You just keep pushing ahead, no matter what. It's like Private Ryan — *you can't stop and say "This guy's dead," or else you're going to be dead.*
—MICHAEL OVITZ

What do you do when you get to work in the morning? Do you have a muffin? A little cup of coffee? Look out the window? Take care of the stuff that somebody might bother you about?

And then, when those things are done, do you kind of kick back, think about women's soccer? Have another cup of coffee?

Then you're not doing what Machiavelli would do, you slug.

Back in 1976, Lou Gerstner was mowing his lawn. I know, it's tough to imagine it now, but that was twenty-five years ago and back then, I guess, Lou Gerstner

mowed his own lawn. It's kind of cute to think about it now. At any rate, he's mowing his own lawn and something terrible happens and there is an accident, and parts of two fingers on his right hand are severed. Things might have been different back then in terms of lawn mowing, but the underlying Gerstner character was already formed, it seems. For, as a surgeon was stitching him back together, he is said to have told the doctor to move more quickly, please. Why? Because he had a business meeting the next day.

Certainly, it was an important meeting. As important as two fingers of your right hand? Only to a true prince.

Bag the fingers. Full speed ahead.

He would kill people, but only if he could feel good about himself afterward

A single death is a tragedy;
a million deaths is a statistic.
—JOSEF STALIN

Okay, Stalin was probably kidding. But as always, he had a serious point underneath. Cutting off a few heads is necessary now and then, and it doesn't pay to get too sentimental about it.

Machiavelli was quite clear about this, too, and a lot of energy has been used up trying to humanize this particular aspect of his philosophy. But it's not that difficult to get behind once emotion and morality are leached out of the decision-making process.

It's a changing world. Mergers. No strong unions. Internet millionaires, some of them quite stupid, driving the economy wacky. Consolidation up the keester. Cutbacks. Bad pensions. Many, many people are confused, and prefer things the way they were, and would

frankly rather die than become a part of the crass, idi-
otic, vicious new world order. Those who feel that way
about it probably should. Die, that is.

"You cannot make a revolution with silk gloves,"
Stalin cracked on another witty occasion. Rulers from
prehistoric days right up to those who implemented
recent improvements in the White House travel office
have found this equally true. And there's nothing
wrong with it. You're the boss. You have the right to
work with people you want to work with. Period.

Machiavelli, for his part, had no trouble advising
his Medici CEO about the wisdom of eliminating enemies of the State for the good of all, particularly in
post-merger situations. The ends in this case—the
transformation of that State to the new and better iter-
ation—truly justify the means—at least for anyone
committed to building a new State.

Not that we don't feel bad about it, and try at the
beginning to soften the inevitable.

Nero, a debauched and murderous loser by the time
he was thirty, tried when he was young to be a very
creditable Caesar, giving away money, food, and land to
many Romans, holding emotional tributes to the guy
who preceded him (very big corporate points), rising to
the position of maybe the most popular lounge singer in
Rome, believe it or not, performing for gigantic crowds—
like Neil Diamond at his height—while at the same time
easing taxes and generally trying to act like a nice dude.

Then he was Caesar for a while.

Near the end there, before his death at thirty-two, he was going out at night by himself to rob and murder innocent citizens returning from an evening at the theater, having sex with many of his family members, including his mother, robbing the estates of his entire social class when he ran out of money . . . stuff like that. When he cruised on his yacht, "he had a row of temporary brothels erected along the shore, where a number of noblewomen, pretending to be madams, stood waiting to solicit his custom," one observer wrote, adding that "he also forced his friends to provide him with dinners; one of them spend 40,000 gold pieces on a turban party, and another even more on a rose banquet."

Sound familiar? I went out with a senior officer last week who made me pick up a dinner for ten bozos, so he wouldn't have to put it on his credit card! More than $2,000! How am I supposed to put that through without exciting the notice of the corporate credit police?

I'll just tell them Maury made me do it. I'm sure that's not the first time they heard that excuse.

Anyhow, we don't have turban parties anymore. Though there was a mid-seventies plane ride from LA to New York I heard about. Several very big record company executives. A couple of girls. Lots of cocaine. All the big lieutenants are up in the front of

the plane. Somebody thinks to check in the back, where the old man is. Guy comes back, his face is ashen. "You'd better get back here," he tells his pals, some of whom work for the senior officer in question. They go back to the rear of the private aircraft and in an alcove they see their extremely dumpy boss, naked, his head buried between the legs of the high school senior he was entertaining. He doesn't appear to be alive. They take him off; they freshen him up. He's not dead. He just passed out in the middle of things. For the rest of their lives, these lucky partygoers have to live with the mental image of their lord and master splayed out like some corrupt Pillsbury doughboy over a teenager at 35,000 feet.

It seems people still do erect an occasional barge on the riverbank.

Where were we? Oh yes. The deaths are for the good of the State. But we get no pleasure in them.

Even master murderer Pol Pot of Cambodia, responsible for the deaths of between 1 and 3 million of his fellow-citizens, saw his actions from the best possible vantage point. "I came to carry out the struggle, not to kill people," he said. That's nice.

But he did kill people! Lots and lots of them. In his long career as a successful executive, this ruthless Machiavellian:

- Coldly changed his persona several times, and his name. Even his family didn't know their little Saloth Sar was actually Pol Pot, the bloody head-count cutter. Many people change their names to establish a new business identity, but it's kind of amusing to find Pol Pot doing it. What was the matter with his original name? Too ethnic?
- Founded the Khmer Rouge, a very violent management team that attempted to completely change the corporate culture of the nation;
- Effected a corporate name change when the transformation of the culture was well underway— from Cambodia to the Kampuchean People's Republic, completely redefining the brand identity of his company;
- Initiated the above-mentioned corporate reorganization that removed all dissident elements and potential dissident elements, as well as possible parents of future dissident elements, as well as all intellectuals, people who wore glasses, people who could read, and others. In doing so, he initiated a dynamic program of massive population relocation and forced labor.

The goal here was to create an agrarian utopia that would be good for everybody. Isn't that an omelet worth the breaking of a few million eggs?

Well, maybe not that many.

Such wretched excesses aside, there is absolutely no doubt that death is the most permanent means of silencing counterrevolutionaries. Most organizations find cuts of between 10 and 15 percent to be optimal to effect cultural change. After that measured action, the living are often willing to take a different attitude about participating. Beyond that, the wheels of the business begin to fall off, and people start to hate you. Pol Pot, for instance, was executed by his own board of directors. Afterward, the press version was considerably cleaned up. This is a fate suffered by many of the CEOs I have known. Although they retired to somewhat more comfortable circumstances.

This should remind us that we are discussing these matters in a business context, where the worst that can happen to somebody (not counting Karen Silkwood) is banishment, and the road to the killing fields ends in the lobby of the unemployment office or, in more elevated cases, the executive search firm hired to smooth the path of the dead into the next life. But the rationale for elimination of cultural undesirables is not materially different in a corporate setting than it was in Kampuchea.

"I believe the principles of structural revolution are the same," Lou Gerstner pointed out in the middle of his positive transformation of IBM. "First, it takes personal commitment on the part of the CEO. This is not a job you can delegate. Second, it takes a willingness to

confront and expel the people and the organizations that are throwing up roadblocks to the changes you consider critical."

Thus every corporate transformation worthy of the name usually must begin with the eradication of some citizens. So do what you must.

Machiavelli would take them out in the following order:

- ⊕ Consultants: They expensively plug gaps that should be filled by cheap staff;
- ⊕ Very old people: They're slower, don't relate to the Internet very well, and can't drink as much as they should;
- ⊕ Very young people: They're way too speedy and ambitious, won't shut up about the Internet, and don't drink as much as they should;
- ⊕ Board members: They're pricey, and an indulgence when too numerous. A small, competent board is the gem in the forehead of Krishna;
- ⊕ Expensive senior officers with a small reporting structure: Give their staff to mid-level officers who are already doing much of the line work;
- ⊕ Assorted losers who nobody likes and no one will miss: I can think of a couple. I'm sure you can too;
- ⊕ Aging boomers who are the backbone of the enterprise;

- People in their thirties, who can talk to people in their twenties;
- Support staff.

Save as many good secretaries as you can. You can't do it without those people. Besides, doesn't yours know an awful lot about you? Do you really want to piss her off?

Look at all those human beings filing out on their way to Siberia—and worse. And you sent them there, you bastard. Sure you feel bad now. But don't worry. It'll get better. Killing people on paper is like anything else. After you've done it for a couple of years, well, I'm not saying it's a stroll in the park, but it's not something that keeps you up at night like it used to.

We'll be dealing with what Machiavelli would do about firing people face-to-face later. That's significantly harder. But as long as you have other people to deliver the bad news to those who have to hear it in person, this part of being a first-class prince is no big whoop.

Relax. You'll live longer.

He would fire his own
mother if necessary

Change is change—it doesn't happen slowly.
The concept of complete satisfaction is like
the concept of truth. You can move toward it,
but you never entirely get there.
—SI NEWHOUSE, CEO, CONDÉ NAST

"You're toast."
—TED TURNER, CEO, TO HIS SON WHILE FIRING HIM

Condé Nast's Newhouse is a famous, outrageous
firer who dispenses with most of the niceties in favor
of speed and finality.

A friend of mine worked for him for many years,
in a very senior position. Her story is not unusual for
that organization, in which people have found out
they were canned by watching gossip Liz Smith on the
5 o'clock news.

This one was particularly brutal. One day she
went out to lunch, an important part of the day for

anyone in the publishing industry, which takes its midday meal as seriously as a bunch of third graders who can't wait to hit the bologna and chips. Lunchtime ends, as it always does, and my friend goes back to her office for a full afternoon of managing and doing and being important, and she finds her door locked. Inexplicably, her key does not fit the lock it has fit quite nicely for several years. In the hallway right outside her office, she suddenly notices, are a bunch of boxes neatly packed. In the boxes are her belongings. She is fired. After a brief talk with Mr. Newhouse, who tells her something about changing direction, she goes home. And that's that.

Every corporation has its own style. My old company used to make up completely fictional new jobs for people so they could keep their dignity during the period they were working off their severance.

At *Esquire* magazine, management at parent Hearst Corporation liked to invite the unsuspecting outgoing editor over to headquarters down the street for the proverbial chat, while they quietly brought his successor in to meet the troops. That always seemed a bit cold-blooded to me.

But all the weird stuff about firing makes absolute sense. It's damned hard to fire another human being face-to-face, which is why you sort of have to congratulate Ted Turner, who took it upon himself to fire his own son from the family business—over dinner.

It's impossible to run a Machiavellian operation without firing people, sometimes a whole lot of people, and sometimes it's going to be right to their faces. Hopefully you'll be a little bit better at it than other people. But there's no good way to do it. That should convey a terrific sense of freedom. Or at least inevitability.

When I attained my current level of corporate activity, I was confronted with several decent people who had been doing quite well in the prior regime. All of them had families. Each needed his or her job. I considered the terrain and saw that nothing would change as long as they were in place. In several instances, they were quite understandably passing snide remarks about me behind my back, barbs that were conveyed by spies who brought them to me like chocolate-covered cherries on a velvet cushion. I rewarded those spies and fired every single one of the people I needed to get out of the way. I practically barfed the night before the first one. The second kind of bugged me, too, particularly when he cried. After that, it was easier.

A few short pointers:

⊕ Let them know you hate them. Let them know it often and clearly. This virtually eliminates their expressions of amazement when you swoop down on them, and cuts down on the puling and pleading. The first person I fired kept saying over

and over again, "You're firing me? You're firing me?" It was pretty intolerable.

- ⊕ Work out a decent cover story. People appreciate it. They're retiring. They're moving on to explore new vistas. They're taking a semester off to study at the Sorbonne. Whatever.

- ⊕ Give them time to get out. It's not going to kill the operation if you don't heave somebody who was once viable out the window like they were an old orange peel.

- ⊕ Don't give them too long, though. I had a soft spot once but it has grown hard. I allowed a person six full months of hanging around being bitter because his wife was about to have a kid. Next time, I'll just give them a few extra bucks and show them the door.

And feel good about yourself. You're doing something that's as important as any other part of the program.

When they were gone, my former associates, I looked about me . . . and it was good. I thoroughly enjoy the absence of each and every one of them, every single day.

Tough? Sure. But the ends were just, you know what I'm talking about?

He would make a virtue out of his obnoxiousness

I love my pussy, it is the complete summation of my life . . . my pussy is the temple of learning.
—MADONNA

Do you mind if I sit back a little? Because your breath is bad—it really is.
—DONALD TRUMP, TO LARRY KING,
ON CNN'S "LARRY KING LIVE"

Princes have their own rules of order, ones that come with the big, hard territory, and they don't care about the laws that govern other people. This ability to act out one's most childish and obnoxious urges is the right of princes, and they exercise it with pleasure. "I'm not gonna claim I don't throw tantrums or scream at people, or that I didn't throw my car phone and smash the windshield," says a Hollywood producer whose most recent movie is as rude as he is. "I happen not to be one of those people who is nice in the abstract," he adds.

This is an important concept for obnoxious people: selective niceness. This guy considers himself to be nice in the specific, but not in general, that is, he's nice to certain people when he wants to be, but most unpleasant and difficult the rest of the time. And he feels good about it.

This is the modern version of the divine right of kings—the ability to be as big a schmuck as you want to be, the pride one feels in flaunting that accomplishment.

It's certainly what Machiavelli would do. I'd like you to start trying it, too. I'm sure there's an obnoxious side to your character. I'm presuming that up until now you've stifled the greater part of it, simply because you're not famous yet.

Well, cut it out. If you have any hope of attaining true power, reach deep for the most abhorrent, offensive parts of your personality and give them some air!

Things to cultivate:

- ✦ Rudeness: Watch people reel back when you put your hand over their faces and push real hard.
- ✦ Greediness: Want something? Take it!
- ✦ Destructiveness: Johnny Depp is a very good actor, but the thing he's most remembered for is trashing hotel rooms. Try to make a name for yourself.
- ✦ Bragging: Donald Trump would be a failed real-estate agent if he didn't have the world's biggest

need to tell everybody how great he is. Everywhere he goes, he marks his spot. I had a dog that did the same thing once, but he did it inside the house and we had to get rid of him. It's harder to do that with people.

- ⊕ Preening: I love how Madonna feels about herself. Long after her voice is gone, her profound and moving statements on the subject will be remembered.

- ⊕ Personal excess: You have bad habits. Some are harmful to yourself, and should still be avoided. But the ones that are harmful to other people can now be celebrated!

You get the picture. The marvelous thing about the human ego is that each one is slightly different. Deep inside you, there's an enormously objectionable force yearning to leap forth and spew toxic goo all over the place. Let it flow!

What Would Machiavelli Do?
✗ ✗ ✗

He would be way upbeat!

I was calm and confident because everything in my work indicated that the economy was going great.

—ABBY JOSEPH COHEN, GOLDMAN SACHS ANALYST, STILL BULLISH AFTER THE 1997 CRASH

"What, me worry?"

**ALFRED E. NEWMAN,
MAD MAGAZINE, ALWAYS BULLISH**

Yeah, baby!

AUSTIN POWERS, INTERNATIONAL MAN OF MYSTERY

A real Machiavellian is happy all the time, except when enraged about something. And why not? He has so much to be thankful for! Cars with drivers. Lots of agreeable people. It's a wonderful life. Sing! Dance! Make merry!

Yeah, right. Because a couple of things *didn't* go exactly the way you wanted them to, did they? So enough of this good mood shit.

What Would Machiavelli Do?
✗ ✗ ✗

He would be satisfied
with nobody but himself

No one has ever met my expectations,
with the exception of my wife.
—LOU GERSTNER

Did you ever notice how substandard things are nowadays? That includes people. People can really suck, particularly when you're depending on them. Even when they do things basically okay, they still suck. You're demanding. You want things:

◈ piping hot
◈ very cold
◈ neat and clean
◈ al dente
◈ now

And everyone, for the most part, lets you down.
Except you. You don't let you down. You know you better than you know anybody else. You know

what you need. You know what you like. You know what worries you and what pisses you off and how to make you feel better. So be good to yourself. Treat yourself better than you do other people.

✗ ✗ ✗

He would treat himself right

*The dead know not any thing, neither have
they any more a reward; for the memory of
them is forgotten. Also their love, and their
hatred, and their envy, is now perished;
neither have they any more a portion for
ever in any thing that is done under the sun.*

—ECCLESIASTES

Are you going to eat the rest of that?

—ANONYMOUS EXECUTIVE,
1999 SALES CONFERENCE

It's a small prince indeed who doesn't pay himself
back on a daily basis for the stress, long hours, and
indignities of life.

I had a chairman once who insisted on flying
coach between New York and Los Angeles. Ron
would talk to you at the gate, and the whole time your
stomach would be churning and your mind spinning
as you calculated how you could possibly slip away
from him to have yourself downgraded. Woe unto the

poor chucklehead who entered the plane without seeing Ron lagging behind to spot who was turning left into first class while he was turning right into the depths of greasy mystery meat and $4 headphones. Boy, how we hated him.

This was a guy who inspired no love, no loyalty, only fear. It wasn't only that he didn't have even one tiny whisker dipped into the milk dish. But that didn't help.

I don't know about you, but I haven't worked for more than fifteen years, dragging myself out of the protoplasm, so I could stand by the curb in the rain of some distant city waving my arms around for a taxicab. Hey. I'm creating value. I'll take the Town Car until somebody tells me I can't. Machiavelli would, too. Or at least he would have ridden along with somebody entitled to one on the way to the next execution.

All truly big hitters applaud a lusty regard for the good things in life. As *Time* magazine observed in a 1997 profile of Miramax honcho Harvey Weinstein, "It has been noted that a family of four could subsist for a month on the crumbs that stick to Weinstein's shirt."

Weinstein's glorious sense of excess is in a great tradition going back as far as ancient Rome, with its jewels and dancing nymphs and vomitoria, and certainly farther, probably to the first cave dweller who

decided he had earned the right to a better fur than the guy in the cave next door.

More recently, the world has opened so wide that even the most mid-level prince or princess can live like a king or a pope.

- ✢ Retreats are held in fabulous locations from Sanibel Island, Florida, to Palm Desert, California. The rooms are huge and cool. Golf is free. The food goes on for miles. Drinks are mandatory. Get your company to organize an "offsite" that you'll be invited to. Call it strategic planning. Man, that's living.
- ✢ Stock options are now penetrating deeper and deeper into organizations, making small windfalls possible that bring within reach new cars, new TVs and stereos, even Winnebagos, if you want one.
- ✢ Personal telephones make everybody feel like a big shot. Treat yourself. It's on the company!
- ✢ Laptops, palmtops, all within reach of the average executive.
- ✢ Many, many people take Town Cars and limos where before only the most senior people could get away with it. Try it couple of times. If nobody bothers you, you're in!
- ✢ Prices for restaurant meals in New York, Los Angeles, San Francisco, and other elite cities have

now reached a plateau where the $100 lunch is not even scrutinized seriously. Have some shaved truffles on your risotto! Good, huh?

⊕ Apartments in big prestigious buildings in major cities go for $10 or $15 million dollars. I know a guy who bought one. He likes it.

If this kind of explosive profligacy doesn't sound familiar, you're not traveling with the right crowd. Interestingly, the good life of fine food, excellent transport, and bottomless pistachios from the mini-bar isn't inconsistent with a frugal monetary strategy for the vast run of the little folk.

Here comes Lou Gerstner again, the grand pooh-bah who whipped IBM into fiscal fitness. Mr. Gerstner, it turns out, relishes a good cigar and fine vodka, and reportedly personally hired a world-class executive chef from his former employer, RJR Nabisco, for $87,500 a year plus a $30,000 signing bonus. This after finding significant headcount in his bloated organization.

For those who need one, the thought process on such seemingly incongruous behavior goes something like this:

Rationales for Self-Indulgence

"I saved the company a lot of money."

"This was an odious job that
took a lot out of me."

"Savings amounted to millions
and millions of dollars."

"Any amount I spend (or make, for that matter)
is chickenfeed in comparison."

"I was here until nearly midnight last night."

"I want my own personal chef and fuck it."

Who could argue with that? Not Machiavelli!

She would view her gender as both a liability and an asset

"It takes a real man to fill my shoes."
—MADONNA

"Ginger had to do everything that Fred did except backwards and in high heels."
—FORMER TEXAS GOVERNOR ANN RICHARDS

You don't need a dick to act like one. But it seems to help.

Not that there aren't plenty of really mean women. Of course there are. I've worked for plenty. One of them, back in the 80s, when senior women were more then exception than the rule, routinely made her support people cry, and there wasn't a person at the rank of vice president or above who was willing to get in her way, particularly after lunch. She did very well, too, for a long, long time. Until she pissed the chairman off. Then she went someplace else, for more money, and I got her job. I'm pretty

sure she's still there, making people avoid her, which is certainly better than the other way around.

I'm still here, too, of course. Not because I'm any less nasty. I'm just better at it than she was. More careful to piss off the right people, you know, and not the wrong ones.

A lot of women have mastered the Machiavellian arts, I don't mean to say they haven't. These pages are full of them. Linda Wachner, tough enough to curl your nose hairs. Martha Stewart, who wrestled her magazine back from the empire of Time Warner because she felt they moved too slow to achieve her lofty goals. Abby Joseph Cohen of Goldman Sachs who, not all that long ago, blew past the sexist doorman at the University Club in New York with the words, "If you want to stop me, go ahead." She got in.

And then there's Hillary Rodham Clinton, who doesn't even look Jewish. But she's perfectly willing to use her new-found heritage to make friends in the New York City area.

So unquestionably, women can and are as potentially bold, pushy, ugly, crass, and manipulative as men. I don't mean to insult anyone by saying otherwise.

But the sad fact is, far too often, way, way too often, you see women who get where they are by hard work and genuine talent and accomplishment, and use nothing more than that to stay on top. Yes,

unfortunately—and I hope you'll correct me if I'm wrong—but there are still many, many women who want to get to positions of power via traditional methods, and without sufficient meanness. This makes them vulnerable to the insanity of others, because they are not sufficiently driven by their own madness.

I feel sorry for such women, because they're just not prepared to be as cruddy as they need to be. Too many are like Sherry Lansing of Paramount, who has the reputation of being "the nicest No in Hollywood." Who needs that kind of reputation? How many men would be proud of it? The Dalai Lama, maybe. But maybe not. I hear he can get really cranky when they screw up his reservation at Spago.

Far too often these days, we hear accomplished, intelligent women mouthing drivel. Take Esther Dyson. She's sort of a genius. She groks the Internet. She sees the future. She writes, consults, goes to formerly Communist nations to help them find a blank floppy disk when they need one. She's at the pinnacle of her game. But is she ravening for more? Looking for ways to crush the opposition and march downfield? Listen to this: "You know," she says, "I'm a real human being. I'm warm. I have friends. I love people, but my maternal instinct is mostly spent on Russia and Eastern Europe, and I love families. I love kids. I don't have my own, so I'm not trying to say people should live like me. They should pick their

own lifestyle and follow it because it suits them."

Isn't that nauseating? They should pick their own lifestyle and follow it because it suits *them?* Very nice. Let's all have some candy apples, for chrissakes. People should pick the lifestyle that suits you. You are the leader. You are the one who must be pleased, not them.

But you see this kind of thing from women again and again. Here's Gerry Laybourne, a very tough operator who keeps on reappearing making more money, always the sign of good Machiavelli work. "Women are best at creating win-win environments," she says, "collaborating, working to make a contribution rather than working to be #1." What a bunch of hooey! On another occasion, I believe I heard her say something about hierarchies and rankings are not what women are all about. This is just bad advice, that's all. It's the kind of stuff that young women trying their best to be vicious don't really need to hear.

At the risk of stating the obvious, here's what both women and men need to know:

- ⊕ That no family considerations transcend business ones for those who want to dominate the cosmos;
- ⊕ That no friends are worth the compulsive pursuit of success, wealth, and power;
- ⊕ That only individuals who are monomaniacal and driven to the exclusion of all else stand a chance of rising to the top;

- That people who try to pour themselves completely into jobs, marriage, and family generally end up going 0 for 3;
- That you should probably get over mourning about the loss of your personal life. Or go home and stay there, after a while. There's really nothing wrong with it, you know. There isn't a day I don't think about it. Then I remember how much fun I'm having and put the idea out of my mind.

Beyond the genderless reach for overwhelming power, there is always sex. We all know what works. I once knew the CEO of one of the biggest conglomerates in the United States. He was the love slave of his senior vice president of finance, an attractive if frightening young woman, who virtually ran the corporation for three years, controlling the company's direction on matters from investment in commercial real estate to contributions to local museums and hospitals. She was lousy at her job, but her job wasn't her job. Her job was Larry.

As Sherry Lansing has said: "I'm not gonna walk around with a bag on my head. If you're a woman, you can give someone a hug. You can talk. You can be nurturing. To deny that part of yourself is not to be operating on all cylinders."

And there is nothing quite so much fun for a male executive than to be in a closed conference

room with a beautiful, accomplished female person operating on all of her cylinders. That's a source of power that can lead to both pleasure and pain, however.

Let's look at that now.

What Would Machiavelli Do?
✗ ✗ ✗

He would use what he's got

*I was one of the few women on Wall Street.
I thought the way of dressing there was just stupid.
I had beautiful long legs. I wore brown velvet hot
pants with brown stockings and brown heels.*

—MARTHA STEWART

*So many CEOs are impeccably logical, but they don't
lift your heart. They rely too much on the way things
should be done. I believe in provocative disruption.*

—CHARLOTTE BEERS,
CHAIRPERSON, J. WALTER THOMPSON

*Charlotte, more than anyone in this business, wants to
seduce. There's something deep about Charlotte, and
also frivolous. She is a woman, a woman, a woman.*

—JEAN-MICHEL GOUDARD,
PRESIDENT, BBDO INTERNATIONAL

I don't know what you've got. But you've got something.

Maybe you're cute. Many people, even if they're

not actually appealing for any other reason, are cute. You can use that.

Perhaps you're ruggedly good-looking, and have some money. That works, too.

On the other hand, you could be truly homely. In that case, get very, very fit and shave your head. That seems to be an excellent option in some industries.

If you believe, however, that you are quite good-looking, congratulations. Believing is possibly all that's really important.

Now go out and be the powerful sexual animal I know you are. But for God's sake, keep it in your pants. The word is *sublimation*, ladies and gentlemen.

What Would Machiavelli Do?
✗ ✗ ✗

He would embrace his own madness

I have existed from the morning of the world, and I shall exist until the last star falls from the heavens. Although I have taken the form of Gaius Caligula, I am all men, as I am no man—and so, I am a god.

—CALIGULA,
ROMAN EMPEROR

Caligula was a nut. He was also the most powerful Roman in the empire until he was murdered. His behavior, throughout his reign, became more and more amusing as he got crazier.

You can do it, too.

A few screwy Caligula highlights: He once ordered several Roman Legions onto the beaches of France and had them collect sea shells in their helmets. As anyone who has ever spent any time on the Riviera can tell you, there are plenty of nice sea shells there. When his employees' helmets were full, the nutty emperor proclaimed that he had won a great victory over the gods of the sea.

That's what I call good spin.

Another time, due to the fact that he was bankrupt, he personally voided all wills that did not name him as an heir. Soon all prominent Romans listed him as principal heir in their wills. Those who regained their health (viewed as an act of treason by the emperor) could expect to receive a gift from him — poisoned food. No kidding.

Caligula couldn't help the fact that he was loony. It was a natural asset that he enjoyed. You'll have to find, cultivate, and celebrate your insanity if you have any hope of ruling others.

It's what Machiavelli would do.

Here are things to look for and grow in your personality on your way to the toppermost position in the food chain:

NARCISSISM: Until you learn to view other people solely as a function of your needs, you will be a short hitter. You have enormous selfishness within you. Let it out. Let it flower. Practice viewing the world around you as the ancients did the universe, with the earth (you) at the center, and the sun, moon, and stars (everything else) rotating around you.

GREED: Because so far you're relatively mediocre, there is an end to your desire. This limits your personal power. You don't have to want everything, that can be a distraction. But you have to want *all*

of *some*thing. If your wanting mechanism loses its direction permanently, and you lose your yen for power and possessions, you may have to fall back on greed for fame unattached to any achievement. It's the smallest kind of greed, and sort of pathetic, but it works for quite a few people it would do me no good to specify.

DELUSIONS OF PERSECUTION: Once you get to a certain level, you're a moron if you don't suffer from this already. Madmen give in to it, and it drives their power engines like high-octane jet fuel.

DELUSIONS OF GRANDEUR: That's right. You're very, very large. You're huge. You're all that. Feel your head float above your body. How lucky the world is to have you in it!

SECRETIVENESS: There is a dark and private place. You must go there a lot. Spend time down there, talking with yourself.

ELATION: On the other hand, what's the point of moping around all the time! Get out there! Mingle! Mix! Hobnob! You're a big cheese!

RIGIDITY: You must play the game that got you here. You must play the game that got you here. You must play the game that got you here.

RAGE: In the meantime, you've got to stave off the nitwits who are determined to bring you down. You won't let them. You'll crush them, hear their bones break, their windpipes snap.

GOLF: This is where it ends. Not with a bang, but with a chip shot that fell just short of the pin and then rolled back in the damnedest way! Kind of curled left and then, I kid you not, took a wicked hop into the bunker! Can you imagine that?

TOTAL BUSINESS EXCELLENCE: To the outside world, you are certifiable. But in a meeting, you are a powerful lighthouse guiding all boats to your harbor. It is your madness that has brought you here, to this fearsome level of functionality.

Why not celebrate it?

What Would Machiavelli Do?
✗ ✗ ✗

He would do what he feels like doing, you idiot

> *Human rights will depend on the time,
> the conditions and . . . the circumstances.
> They will always be in step with the
> revolution and its principles.*
> —SADDAM HUSSEIN

In other words, there aren't any.

The ruler of Iraq is only one dramatic example of the tendency of successful Machiavellis to do what they want to do and ask questions . . . well, never, actually. Frederick the Great of, what was it? Germany? Anyhow, his basic philosophy was encapsulated in his famous statement, "I have an agreement with my people. They can say what they want. I can do what I want." He can be counted a liberal ruler because he didn't mind letting people say what they want. Within reason, of course.

Doing whatever you want is necessary 1) for the establishment of your personal style and happiness,

and 2) to get what you want. See? In this case:

Doing = Getting.

Put in mathematical terms, this boils down to: $D = G^2$, where D is the amount of Doing (in energy units), and is equal to G, the amount of Getting, squared. It shows that any amount of doing results in an exponential amount of getting. If you're doing all that, you might as well be doing what you want.

Absolutely doing what you want in all circumstances will also make others fear you, because they know that when it comes right down to it, you don't give a shit.

And not giving a shit is big mojo.

Not giving a shit is made up of three parts:

1. Not being afraid of what other people think;
2. Not caring about their feelings;
3. Keeping your eyes on the prize.

But if I have to teach you how not to give a shit, you're in worse trouble than I thought. You know what to do. It's inside you already, muffled by your cowardice and mediocrity. Reach down and find *your* not giving a shit. There. Now haul it out and put it to work.

It isn't that easy, is it.

The first obstacle is that many of you just don't really know what you want at any given moment. This makes you losers.

Real princes know what they want each and every minute of the day, and most of the night, too, when they're not sleeping, which they don't do very well anyhow.

But they're not that different than you. They don't know what they want out of life. They don't necessarily know what they're going to want tomorrow morning, or the next day, or even in two hours, really. They just know what they want right now. And they go after it.

You can, too. See everyone as a function of whether they can help you get what you want *right now.* Those who help you can live. Those who do not help you can die. That's clarity. Clarity is what you want, dude.

To attain that clarity, make sure you have what you want in focus at every moment. See it as an exercise. Things you may want to do right now:

1. Get the numbers from the mid-Atlantic region, but only if they're good;
2. Study your personal investments for a while;
3. Eat something fast while standing up;
4. Walk out of this stupid meeting, which is an enormous waste of time;
5. Kick Armbruster's ass;
6. Make Weaver cry;
7. Have a big fat stogie;
8. Get Nordlinger to fire Niedermeier;

9. Scream at Backus;
10. Hit the can;
11. Kill Vreeland;
12. Chase Barber around the desk.

Only the last one should give you pause. Even the largest prince can get in serious trouble for that kind of thing these days. But believe me, most people don't, so who knows. Maybe it's worth a try.

Go! Do! And don't worry about ruffling others' feathers. It is a little known fact, for example, that in addition to his other achievements, Saddam Hussein is also an attorney. I would venture to say that he's probably a pretty good one, particularly in his home court, although it's hard to see how he could be better than, say, Bert Fields, who represented Jeffrey Katzenberg in his suit against Michael Eisner. There's a guy you don't want to hear on the other end of a phone, unless he's inviting you to Spago.

It's possible that Fields worked harder than Hussein did to get his law degree, however, for in addition to his connections, Saddam simply had *no intention of allowing failure to occur*. He wanted what he wanted and went out to get it. Anyone who doubts his determination should consider the fact that when he showed up to take the bar exam, it seems he arrived carrying, among other things, his pistol. He kept it within view while he took the exam, the little point of

his tongue presumably peeping out the corner of his mouth as he worked with pencil and eraser to make sure his exam paper was neat and 100 percent correct.

He passed!

I'm not saying that he didn't know Iraqi law, if that's not an oxymoron. But the visible pistol didn't hurt. Keep yours at the ready.

What Would Machiavelli Do?
✗ ✗ ✗

He would say what he felt like saying

> *I've learned that great wealth*
> *isn't nearly as good as average sex.*
> —TED TURNER, SPEECH BEFORE THE
> AMERICAN SOCIETY OF MAGAZINE EDITORS

Ted Turner will say anything. Whatever appears in his brain has a pretty fair chance of making it out of his mouth. At a speech at the Washington Press Club, he regaled a group of journalists with a long harangue on the subject of genital mutilation in Africa. People were pretty interested.

There is a legend in the business. Back when he was looking for a top content guy at CNN, Ted met with Rick Kaplan, formerly of ABC News. Kaplan is tall, about six feet, five inches or so. "Wow!" Turner is said to have exclaimed when he met him. "You're the biggest Jew I've ever seen!" Kaplan got the job, as we know, and Turner has been Kaplan's, er, rabbi, through one crisis in journalistic confidence and one ugly feud with the Graf Zeppelin of business journalism, Lou Dobbs.

At other times, Turner he has remarked:

⊕ that Chinese political dissidents "asked for it at Tiananmen Square";
⊕ that Christianity was a religion for losers;
⊕ of the people who committed suicide in Keds with psycho-guru William Applegate, "There are too many people anyway; it's a good way to get rid of a few nuts; you gotta look at it that way."

All of these statements share a common attribute. They're all funny. Ted Turner makes humor work for him better than any man in business.

What have you got going on in the darkest recesses of your highly individual mind? Hmm? Think about it.

And the next time something feels like it wants to come bubbling up from there, let it out of the front gate.

Or don't, and remain what you are.

What Would Machiavelli Do?
✗ ✗ ✗

He would delegate all crummy tasks— except the ones he enjoys

Just do it.
—NIKE AD

Pls. Hndl.
—ANONYMOUS BUCKSLIP

You don't have to be a powerful prince to start on the process of getting other people to do the stuff you don't wanna do.

Something lousy on the horizon? Got tossed to you by somebody up above doing his Machiavellian duty? There are as many ways to get rid of it as there are people around you to exploit. It's amazing how many people will simply do what you tell them to do if you sound serious and determined. They may resent you. But guess what. Fuck 'em!

Don't forget, by the way, to reclaim the project you're handing off once it's almost finished. You want credit for it once it's clear that it's going to be a success.

What Would Machiavelli Do?
✗ ✗ ✗

He wouldn't exactly seek the company of ass-kissers and bimbos, but he wouldn't reject them out of hand, either

You look mahvelous!
—BILLY CRYSTAL

Who doesn't like to hear nice things about themselves, especially during a long, hard day of stomping, thumping, grabbing and, managing?

Accepting good sucking up is the mark of a true leader. People have to show their love to you some way. Let them, bless their tiny little hearts.

On the other hand, save some room for people who show their love by telling you the truth, too. As long as they're not critical of you.

You don't need that.

He would respond poorly to criticism

*When a general gave unwanted advice
at a meeting, Saddam ordered him to stand,
and shot him six times.*

—FIRST-PERSON ACCOUNT,
SADDAM HUSSEIN WEB HIT

You know what? Nobody likes to be criticized. And the bigger you are, the less you like it.

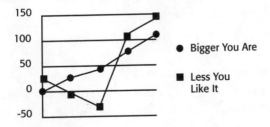

So don't put up with it, chump. If they feel like there's something you need to know about your behavior or performance, so be it. Let them talk. But make them pay.

He would carry a grudge until the extinction of the cockroach

I guess I fucked you once, so I understand.
—MICHAEL OVITZ

A grudge is resentment, held over time. It is not a vendetta, which must be expunged with blood, or a beef, which can be mended with rational action. It's a niggling thing, a little nut that can be tucked away into your cheek for later consumption. Collect a few.

Then crack 'em.

When Bernie Brillstein became head of Lorimar Film Entertainment in early 1987, Mike Ovitz was not told in advance. This was wrong. In his role as titanic force in the industry, someone should have done him the courtesy of a heads-up.

"I lost face," Ovitz recalled later in *Vanity Fair*. "So I decided that Lorimar would be the last stop on the train when we went out with material." This sound dirty to you? Vindictive? Unnecessary?

Get out of this book. Come back when you're ready.

And life is long, you know? Wait. Take it easy. One day, your grudge will pay off. They always do. And then? Well, you know. They say revenge is a dish best eaten cold. Of course, you can eat it hot, too. It's particularly good with croutons.

Ovitz is a clearly a master of this aspect of personal power. When he left Disney several years ago, after a rocky if lucrative stint that was certain to generate some profound grudges on all sides, he reportedly met his former Creative Artists Agency partner, Ron Meyer, for lunch. At the meal, Meyer said he was thinking of buying a Malibu estate that once belonged to Berry Gordy, the founder of Motown. Two days later, Meyer decided to buy the property, only to find out that Ovitz, based on the information he had gotten from his former partner at lunch, had purchased it the day before. After the intercession of peacekeeper Barry Diller (!), Ovitz agreed to sell the land back to Meyer, but held onto it for a few weeks more because, as he told *Vanity Fair*, "I wasn't too pleased with certain things that a lot of Ron's friends, mainly David Geffen, were saying about me."

That's good grudge work. For this reason, for a long time it was tough to find anyone who would speak freely about Michael Ovitz, even in private conversation, and the court press remains unusually

polite in its proctological examinations. In fact, the awed hush that still falls over media people when his name comes up is second in depth and resonance only to that enjoyed by the ultimate object of fear and respect, Martha Stewart, whose acolytes would no more besmirch her name with gossip than followers of the late Lubovitcher Rebbe would have been caught yakking about their man behind his back.

And that's a good thing. Why should folks be able to talk without consequences, anyhow?

What Would Machiavelli Do?
✗ ✗ ✗

He would lie, when it was necessary

I didn't inhale.
—BILL CLINTON

The truth is your servant, not your master.

What is the truth, anyway? Does any of us really know what's true? And is truth an absolute? Can't things be sort of true? A little bit true? True in a deeper sense? True enough for military work? True for me, not for you? All too true? Of course they can. Particularly if have the personal power to make other people see the truth your way.

Thus, we see that as an individual becomes more powerful, his need to employ the truth follows suit, until we reach the point, among really big princes, where everything they say is true simply because they say it. As Richard Nixon once observed to David Frost: "When the president does it, that means that it is not illegal."

What might be a lie to other men is, to the prince, simply one more aspect of his right to control the environment in which he operates. And moral judg-

ments are not only pointless, but kind of rude, don't you think?

The list of accomplished liars is long and impressive. It doesn't pay to name them all. It would, in fact, be easier to name those who did not lie when it became necessary, although that might be impossible. Those who do not lie do not succeed, and therefore remain unknown. Okay, maybe George Washington, but after that?

Creative truth tellers from the recent past include:

- ⊕ Cigarette companies who still keep on telling us that they are aware of no evidence to link smoking with cancer;
- ⊕ Senior officers who tell the media that their company is not for sale when it is;
- ⊕ Senior officers who tell the media (off the record, just between you and me) that their company is about to do a gargantuan business deal, when it isn't;
- ⊕ Kenneth Starr leaking propriety information to the news media about his confidential investigation, then investigating people who complained about it:
- ⊕ Sid Blumenthal, who complained about Kenneth Starr to the media, then said he didn't;
- ⊕ Saddam Hussein, who wants to keep on producing weapons of mass destruction;
- ⊕ Slobodan Milosevic.

And so many others. The key to success in all these individuals is that *they believe the lies they tell.* This conveys a powerful sense of conviction, and makes weak people trust them. Lying for a good business reason has become so prevalent that they had to invent a new, less censorious word for it. They call it *positioning,* and people get paid good money to do it, lucky for me.

You can separate the amateurs from the big boys when they get caught. Serious players who are busted for what other people might consider a lie feel no shame.

They were just doing what Machiavelli would do.

Bill Clinton has perhaps been the most amazing practitioner of truth management in public life. He's had to be. Beset by enemies willing to use any tool to do him in, he let the truth out like a fly fisherman plays out a line, delicately, artfully, with infinite finesse, never emitting more truth than necessary, struggling mightily to tell us what he could without admitting defeat.

Thanks to his dexterity, his adversaries did not succeed, even though the entire media-industrial complex was on their side, even after many an admission was squeezed from him, because at every step he did not do the easy thing and dribble the truth all down his shirtfront. He had the courage to *manage* the truth, defining it, parsing it, making it serve him. "It depends on what your definition of 'is' is," he told his tormentors, and

many Americans shook their heads in wonder, not only at the ridiculousness of the statement, but at the tenacity and toughness of a true Machiavelli who would not, could not, let his enemies use their version of the truth to defeat him.

"I'm trying to be honest with you," he said, "and it hurts me."

Yes. The truth does hurt. And in many cases, it kills. Don't let that truth happen to you.

Manage it.

What Would Machiavelli Do?
✗ ✗ ✗

He would be proud of his cruelty and see it as strength

I'm the kind of guy who sucks the air out of the room.
—STEVE FLORIO, PRESIDENT AND CEO,
CONDÉ NAST PUBLICATIONS

I've left bodies in my path, believe me, because I'm aggressive and sometimes I'm insensitive.
—MICHAEL OVITZ

Say it loud: You're mean and you're proud.

There's nothing wrong with it. Accept that. There are no winners who aren't hard as a rock inside. When the time comes, you have to be ready, and you have to let yourself off the hook about it. Things to feel good about as you stalk about, crushing the world around you:

⊕ Somebody has to do hard stuff. That's a burden, not something you've chosen. Some people have greatness thrust upon them. That's you!

⊕ A lot of people would shrink from what you have

to do *every day*. You, on the other hand, have courage and a real strong stomach. Good for you!

⊕ This whole enterprise would fall apart without you. By taking these tough steps (whatever they are) you're ensuring the future for everybody. Hats off to you!

⊕ What's "mean," anyhow? The world is mean. You're a part of the world. That's sad, but true. Not everybody can live with the truth. You can. Bravo for you!

⊕ Most great men and women were very mean. We can include:

  ⊕ All those kings and queens in Shakespeare, like Macbeth (killed his boss and his enemy's kids), a bunch of Henrys, Richard III (more dead kids), Hamlet (not mean enough until the very end and therefore very annoying);

  ⊕ Andrew Carnegie (whose goons shot a bunch of working people dead but who is now mostly remembered as a big philanthropist with a famous concert hall named in his honor);

  ⊕ Henry Ford (big anti-Semite and Nazi enthusiast now remembered as a slightly eccentric genius who invented mass production);

  ⊕ Joseph McCarthy (initiated the witchhunts of the 1950s, put a bunch of people out of work because of their political beliefs, ran semi-totalitarian operation reminiscent of Stalin

show trials, invented Roy Cohn);

- ✦ Kenneth Starr (initiated the witchhunts of the 1990s, put an entire democratically elected government out of business for more than two full years, ran semitotalitarian operation reminiscent of McCarthy show trials, invented Monica Lewinsky);
- ✦ Neutron Jack Welch (very competitive head of GE, takes no prisoners, nut about Quality, created an entire culture of people dedicated to smashing their opposition in the most unkind and public way possible);
- ✦ Barry Diller (famous temper, let's not go into it, I don't want to get in trouble with him);
- ✦ Lou Gerstner (went ballistic on *Fortune* magazine when they wrote that he has a tendency to go ballistic on people);
- ✦ Dick Snyder, head of Simon & Schuster, who reportedly used to throw things at people. In fact, a lot of princes throw things. I had an editor once who used to buy cheap reading glasses at the local pharmacy explicitly for the purpose of later throwing them at people's heads. It made them perform a lot better.

That leaves out all the most obvious mean and successful dictators throughout history, like Napoleon, Hitler, Stalin, Mao, the czars (or the tsars, depending on

how you look at it), Milosevic, Mobutu, and George Steinbrenner (before he got all squishy). Believe me, none of them lost one wink of sleep over what they had to do.

So suck it up and have as much fun as you can while you're getting the job done. A lot of really bad things lie ahead of you. If you're not going to enjoy them, you might as well not get started.

He would kick ass and take names

You're eunuchs. How can your wives stand you.
You've got nothing between your legs.

—LINDA WACHNER, PRESIDENT, CEO,
AND CHAIRMAN, WARNACO INC.,
TO HER EXECUTIVES

You can't be too insulting. Let me put that another way. You can be as insulting as you like. Isn't that great?

All your life, you tried to live by certain rules of politeness and order. Now you can toss all that out the window. The Machiavellian leader sends a very clear message to his or her troops: Do good. Or be humiliated.

There are two parts to this:

Kicking ass.
Taking names.

Let's have a look at each.

Kicking Ass

This is not simple punishment for something done wrong. This is an immediate thumping for what has generated displeasure in the prince. It must be done publicly, and hurt the offending executive . . . in the ass.

Think about that for a minute. How do we describe the very worst people and things that we encounter on a day to day basis? As a "pain in the ass," that's right. Your job, then, is to inflict just such a first-class pain. In the ass, of course.

What is it like to get kicked in the ass? Is it the same as getting shot in the head? Clearly not. Is it like being punched in the gut? Not at all. How about a smack in the nose? Is it like that? I think not. No, a kick in the ass is something special. It propels you forward, reeling. It makes you look silly. It hurts your pride as much as your ass, although it certainly does hurt your ass, no doubt about that. Come to think of it, when was the last time your ass hurt that way?

When Mommy or Daddy spanked you, that's when! See? Ass kicking is spanking for adults. It's not a death blow. But the recipient shouldn't be able to sit down for a week.

As Ms. Wachner's castrating comment suggests, there are no holds barred when a first-class ass-kicking is on tap. You have the power to say and do

anything you wish, as long as it inflicts pain and humiliation.

Perennial solutions include:

- ⊕ Calling attention to people's stupidity;
- ⊕ Criticizing their looks;
- ⊕ Cutting them off curtly when they speak;
- ⊕ Lecturing them about the nature of loyalty;
- ⊕ Threatening their jobs;
- ⊕ Cutting their budgets to the point where they have to stop having expensive lunches;
- ⊕ Kicking them out of the room.
- ⊕ Firing their favorite employees so that they have to work harder and feel guilty while doing so.

Those are just a few. I'm sure you can think of more.

Ass-kicking takes personal knowledge of the individual involved, and insight into which part of your foot will connect most squarely on the biggest amount of ass.

As with anything, practice makes perfect.

Taking Names

The name-taking phase immediately follows, generating paranoia among those associated with the person whose ass was just kicked.

The thought process is simple—one kicked ass was not enough, we need more! Who are they? We need their names! Go get 'em!

This combination—the kicking ass part, followed by the spreading of fear associated with the taking of names—is far more effective than either half practiced alone. As with all great multilevel strategies, the total impact is more than the sum of its parts.

And it boils down to a rudimentary concept: People know that you can and will hurt them. And when you're done hurting them? You're perfectly capable of hurting their friends.

Linda Wachner does the ass/names thing in the garment business, where it's tough to get through a day without somebody bursting an aneurysm in your face. One time, it is said, she collared the company's new president, who had been there only a few weeks:

"Have you fired anyone yet?" she inquired as, presumably, his testicles shriveled up to the size of walnuts.

"No," he replied.

"Well," Wachner said, "you'd better start firing people so they'll understand you're serious."

Do you think he did?

He would permanently cripple those who disappoint him

Punishment is not for the benefit of the sinner but for the salvation of his comrades.

—GEORGE PATTON

Beyond simple ass-kicking lies the land where big demands are made and failure is not acceptable.

Not long ago, there was a popular general manager at a business I know about. Everybody liked Jim. His managers felt he gave them a new sense of direction. The community appreciated the outreach he was trying to effect. He took a high profile at the plant, where for the first time people felt they could talk to senior management. He looked good in a suit. There was only one thing wrong. Sales sucked.

Three quarters went by like that, and then, at the top of his popularity and power, the corporation took Jim out. It was his immediate superior who did it. But it was the top executive in Chicago who made sure it was done. Call him Bob. Plant managers around the

nation took note. I'm not saying numbers are better in that business. But line management is certainly a lot more nervous.

And that's always a good thing.

This same business runs a big sales organization out of St. Louis. They do very well, year after year. But growth is in the low single digits. Bob wants growth to be in the high single digits, and therefore, so do Bob's lieutenants. So one day the entire top tier of sales management went away out there. Their combined experience in the business came to more than a hundred years. Now they're bye-bye. Word was they spent a fair amount of time schmoozing buyers at lunch, sometimes drinking more than one cocktail at midday during that effort. Sometimes there weren't a lot of buyers around, but they had a couple of cocktails anyhow. Whatever. Management was disappointed. New guys were called for.

Growth is better now.

To be effective, correction must be swift and sure. There was once this fellow who joined our organization from the West Coast. Sleek little guy. Trim. Tiny bullet head. Very condescending. Knew everything. He was hired to revamp our strategy on a number of key issues and blah blah blah. He was hired as a corporate politician, that's all.

So this smart, overpaid, sassy dude goes into his first major meeting with our then-CEO, Mark. He spends a

fair amount of time shitting on the efforts of the corporation to date, and making a lot of noises about revamping the entire landscape and not with a spade and shovel, either, no, with some very heavy machinery. In the process, he evinces almost no particular knowledge of our company, and also manages to poop on the parades of everyone sitting around the table, including Mark's.

After the meeting, Mark was standing in the hallway with the president of the company, just two princes hobnobbing, and on his way down the hall back to his office, Mark turns, like he had a small afterthought, and says, "Oh, by the way, Lenny. That new guy? You may want to see him again for some reason, but I don't want to, ever. If he's at a meeting, I don't need to be there."

Lenny wrestled with the beast that night, and didn't sleep a wink. He had just hired an executive for big money who was now persona non grata with the chairman. He could work with the guy. He could try to brief him, rehabilitate him. Cultivate his best qualities. Work on a way to help him start over. Try to salvage something from the mess.

Or not. Lenny got to work early the next day, called the arrogant little fellow into his office, and said, "You know, Barry, I could lie and say this was off to a rocky start and that we needed to work on things to get back on the right foot, but you know, I don't want to. You're out."

I've heard of quick and lucrative exit visas from corporate America. But that one was the swiftest and richest.

So I guess this story has a happy ending, huh?

He would torture people until they were only too happy to destroy themselves

Hell is other people.
—JEAN-PAUL SARTRE

Not everyone is like my old boss Lenny. Many mean people find it tough to fire people outright. It's too intimate an act, too fraught with personal peril. They just torture people until they want to kill themselves or, on occasion, force them to drive themselves until their hearts pop.

There are so many ways you can torture a person, once you have them in captivity:

SLEEP DEPRIVATION: An old brainwashing trick. Keep employees at the office for no good reason other than you "may want to see them" until they begin crying for their dinners. Waking them up very early with screaming imprecations works well, too.

UNCERTAINTY: Who is buying us? Who will be my boss? What does Marv think of me? Will I make it to retirement? Will my pension be discontinued? What am I going to do if my job is eliminated? Good questions—for which you provide no answers.

HOLDING THEIR FEET TO THE FIRE: Double-digit growth must be achieved, even in a down market.

PUSHING THEIR NOSES AGAINST THE GRINDSTONE: Produce value! Mush! Mush!

MAKING THEM EAT DIRT: It tastes bad. But I want you to eat it in front of all these nice people. Have some more. Good boy.

DRIPPING ON THEIR HEADS UNTIL THEY GO CRAZY: The Chinese invented it, and it works. Can't you get that project in on time? Can't it cost less? Can't you get it in on time? Can't it cost less? Can't it cost less? Huh? Huh?

SQUEEZING: I want more from you ladies and gentlemen! What do I pay you for?!

PULLING THEM APART FROM ALL DIRECTIONS: You'll need to be in San Francisco, New York, and your daughter's wedding, all at the same time next Sunday.

SURPRISING THEM WITH FRIGHTENING DEVELOPMENTS: The deal is falling through! No deal, no bonuses! Save the deal, Brewster! I'm relying on you! What? You can't!? You stink! You stink!

ALTERNATING KINDNESS AND CRUELTY UNTIL
THEY DON'T KNOW WHERE THEY'RE COMING FROM:
I love you. Now get out of here.

And so on. What does it look like?

Super-garmento Linda Wachner once called in one of her senior managers from out of town. After meeting with him, she declared she needed to speak with him once more before their discourse was done. The man reports he cooled his heels in the New York office for three days before she deigned to see him again. That encounter lasted less than two minutes, after which he was sent home.

Another executive told *Fortune* that Wachner telephoned him no less than thirty-one times over his Thanksgiving holiday. By the end of the weekend he had quit.

The point is, sometimes you don't want to make it easy for people. Sometimes you want them to show a little initiative and take their own lives.

Either way, you win.

What Would Machiavelli Do?
✗ ✗ ✗

He would feast on other people's discord

Business is conflict. That's the creative process.
You don't get excellence by saying yes.
You get love, but you don't get excellence.
—RICHARD SNYDER, PUBLISHING CEO

How do you get people to do what you want? More importantly, how do you force people who work for you to be loyal to you, only to you, and not develop some sniveling affection for one another that transcends their fealty to you, their god?

You set them at one another. And watch them rip out one another's throats in an effort to please you better.

They call it "creative tension," which is as good a name as any for a making normally productive people turn into vicious, snarling engines.

Following is a chart that demonstrates the measured performance of people functioning both without and with a highly charged, super-competitive environment in which they are pitted against their fellow workers.

PERFORMANCE WITH AND
WITHOUT RUTHLESS COMPETITION

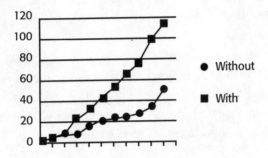

Try these things to help them get on each others'
nerves:

⊕ Invite select associates to some meetings, while
  excluding others. Do not be consistent. Create a
  continuous sense of uncertainty in people around
  you about whether they are in or out.
⊕ Assign the same task to different people without
  telling them you have done so. Let them find it
  out for themselves.
⊕ Talk about others to their peers. Sometimes you
  can compliment them, sometimes you can bitch
  about them. Create the feeling in all people that
  you're willing to talk about them behind their
  backs, and pretty candidly, too.

- Be very clear in discussions that someone else's priority has effectively killed those of their peers. "I would have time/money/interest in that, Fred, but Betty's project got in first/looks better/is more interesting."
- Praise people publicly in a way that shames others. "If all of you had Bob's moxie/brains/contacts, we'd all be doing a lot better," you might say. Direct praise that does not involve the denigration of others is virtually worthless.

What you want is an atmosphere of high-energy, cutthroat rivalry among those who surround you. This focuses all activity in the neighborhood on your approval. All action, no matter how smart or lucrative, is a valued only if it meets with your strong approval and places the actor one notch up on his associates.

What Would Machiavelli Do?

✗ ✗ ✗

He would make you fear for your life

I needed to wear a diaper on that day.
I was very scared.
—VANILLA ICE

Somewhere along the line, Shug Knight, the founder of Death Row records and no small gangsta himself, decided that one of the artists he represented was owed a piece of the song "Ice Ice Baby," which had been recorded by the one successful white rapper, Vanilla Ice.

The song was a big hit. It was making a lot of money.

So at some point, Mr. Ice found that everywhere he went, Mr. Knight was there, with a couple of friends. Mr. Ice would be sitting at a restaurant or club, and he'd look over at a table across the room, and sure enough, there would be Mr. Knight, who always went around armed. Mr. Knight would flip Mr. Ice a little wave, just to say peekaboo, I see you.

The message in the greeting was clear, and anything but friendly. I know where you are. I can get to you whenever I like.

This went on for a while, with Mr. Ice getting more and more nervous about his personal safety, feeling more and more exposed.

Then one day, his subject well-softened now, Mr. Knight and several of his associates sort of kidnapped Mr. Ice and invited him in one way or another to take a business meeting in a hotel room downtown. During the course of that meeting, Mr. Knight and his team found it beneficial to hang Mr. Ice outside the hotel room window for a discussion of the finer points of their position.

Convinced about the seriousness of Mr. Knights intentions, Mr. Ice handed over a significant portion of the rights to the song in question. End of meeting.

He would be loyal to the people who could put up with all this

> *I've never fucked over anyone*
> *who I thought was for me.*
> —SCOTT RUDIN

You'd think with all the rough edges, the meanness, the self-centered quality of his or her daily life, the prince would also be cold-bloodedly detached from the bonds that tie more normal people to each other.

No way. If anything, the true prince is fanatical about establishing and maintaining an insane level of loyalty, loyalty unto death. And that kind of tie goes both ways.

After he had made one of his famous escapes from the law, John Dillinger was a free man, hiding in plain sight across America. Yet he took incredible risks and time out from his extensive schedule of bank-robbing to return to the jail in Indiana where the rest of his gang was incarcerated. In the dead of night, as he had promised them, he threw several large bags of weapons

over the prison wall, making possible his subordinates' hasty exit from that particular hotel. He didn't have to do it. They were in there for the duration, and he was free. But he was loyal. And in the end, they paid back that loyalty with their blood.

His loyalty was proof of the Machiavellian force of his management. Smaller princes do not have it.

Master doofus/criminal Martin Frankel built a huge, crooked empire swindling insurance companies, investors, and the Vatican. A bad guy, certainly. In the meantime, however, he was very good to his people. When he escaped the country with two of the many women who ministered to his rather unprepossessing, geeky self, he left behind a hilarious to-do list (number one was the reminder to "launder money") and a burning file cabinet full of incriminating documentation. It was clear he was in a hurry. He also, according to the *Wall Street Journal*, took the time to send a handwritten fax to his longtime aide, David Rosse, which stated, "I, Marty Frankel, used David Rosse's name without his permission or knowledge."

He didn't have to get his associate off the hook. It didn't buy him anything. It was just the act of a loyal boss to a subordinate who had done a creditable job in pursuit of excellence, no matter how questionable.

In addition to touching gestures like the exculpatory fax, Mr. Frankel also sprung for a great bunch of

hard goodies for his people (most of them attractive women) who made his work possible on a daily basis, buying them homes, shopping sprees at Neiman Marcus and Saks, cars, toys, gems, and money. When he got away, the authorities believe, he made it possible for his associates to make off with bonuses for their labors in the form of jewels, cash, and other shavings from the huge mountain of stolen assets.

If I seem to be saying that Machiavelli would buy the loyalty of his people, this is only partially true. Like, 90 percent. It should cost less, obviously, if you've got some other way of making people love you. For the moment, let's make believe you don't.

Of all the bosses for whom I've worked, it's the ones who gave me cars and options who still make me mist up with genuine, affectionate reminiscence. Not long ago, I went to a dinner with a bunch of guys I used to work with. We still gather as a group once or twice a year, for old times' sake, and get loaded, see where we've all got to. The bond is held strong by the fact that we all still bear tremendous affection and loyalty (with no context now) for the chairman of our little group, who has now moved on to other things. Last time we met, there was still, after several years, a massive cloud of love in the room, fueled by memory and a significant quantity of gin. I stood, sort of, on the street with a couple of buds afterward, and said goodnight.

"Walt looks good," said Morgenstern.

We all agreed that Walt certainly did.

"It's great to be with him again," said Rafferty.

We all agreed it was. We were quiet then for a while, thinking about the way time goes and how nothing lasts in business except, maybe, this.

"Guy got me my first car," said Morgenstern. Then we all lit cigars and went for a nightcap we didn't need.

Unless you can generate that kind of loyalty in others, you will remain the worm you are today. So:

- ✦ Give them raises—what's the couple of grand going to mean to you? But it means the world to them. You are what you pay for.
- ✦ Give them promotions—early and often. They will die for you if you do.
- ✦ Give them perks—stock options cost nothing at the number and level we're talking about. Cars are a little more complicated, but generate genuine, deep emotion in the recipient. Good expense accounts loosen the connections to non-business life most people enjoy. When they're spending your money, you own them. So be liberal.

And between blows, goads, pressure, manipulation, exploitation you visit on others—tell them you love them. Tell them in one way or another, and tell

them a lot. After a while, you know what? It will start to be true.

From that point on, stand back and watch your people burn with a white-hot loyalty ten times the size and intensity of yours.

What Would Machiavelli Do?
✗ ✗ ✗

He would have no patience for anyfuckingbody

My patience is now at an end.
—ADOLF HITLER, IN 1938

I am not very long on patience.
—LINDA WACHNER

Damn right I get in battles. I've got no patience, none, for indecision or sloth. I am not by nature a team player. I try hard to remain unimpressed by that which is unimpressive, so I get into a lot of arguments.
—SCOTT RUDIN

You know . . .

I could go on about this but screw it. Patience is for pussies. We don't need to spend a lot of time on this concept, do we?

Good. Let's move on.

What Would Machiavelli Do?

✗ ✗ ✗

He would screw with people's weekends, wedding plans, open-heart surgery . . .

You're not going away next week, are you?
—FORMER EXECUTIVE, HEARST CORPORATION

So what if they have a vacation? You need them here. Unless you're determined to be a second-rate wimp, you're going to need to insist your needs are met before theirs are.

It gets a little rougher when you need to mess with weddings and funerals, but I've seen it done. I've seen people brought back from Montana, where they were camping with their families. I've seen a woman hauled in for a conference call two days after she had a baby.

They were needed. And they came, called inevitably by the one leader in the organization who was willing to do what Machiavelli would do. They didn't like it. Who says they have to like it?

What Would Machiavelli Do?
✗ ✗ ✗

He would put it in your face

Barry came up, and we shot the breeze for a while. And then he leaned in close and said, very casually, "We're going to announce that we're putting The Simpsons *against* The Cosby Show." *It made me feel sick to my stomach.*

—BRANDON TARTIKOFF,
ON BARRY DILLER

Barry Diller is the acknowledged titan of this kind of thing, but only because he tends to brag on himself all the time. I know some world-class in-your-face men that could show him how it was done. They're just more modest about it.

There are four steps by which those who do not naturally get in other people's faces can learn to do so.

1. Step into the face. You can't get into somebody's face from the side. If you try, you will only end up getting into the side of their face, not directly into their face.

2. Don't stay in the face too long. This gives the
   other face a chance to collect itself and consider
   coming back into your face.
3. But don't leave until the job is done. Keep up
   good intensity until the other face is as close as
   it's going to get to complete collapse.
4. Then withdraw. And don't come back into the
   same face again for a while.

Faces get tougher when you keep on going into the
same ones over and over again, and the tactic becomes
less effective and more purely annoying.

What Would Machiavelli Do?

He would realize that loving yourself means never having to say you're sorry

I would not exist if corporate America did their job.
—"CHAIN SAW" AL DUNLAP

I'm intense, competitive, focused, blunt, and tough, yes. That's fair. I'm guilty.
—LOU GERSTNER

I gotta be me.
—SAMMY DAVIS, JR.

It's easy. Princes never do anything wrong, so they never need to apologize. When they're right they're right. And when they're wrong they're right. That's a lot more fun than occasionally feeling that what you do is wrong, and worse, feeling the need to eat crow.

That Machiavelli would *not* do.

Donald Trump, for instance, grossed out all New Yorkers when he blew up the beautiful art deco friezes that had festooned the Bonwit Teller building a few years back. "Who cares," Trump told reporter Marie Brenner when she raised the point. "Let's say I had given that junk to the Met. They would have just put [it] in their basement."

He was right, see? That stuff was junk and needed to be thrown away. He was doing the city a favor. End of story.

One of my favorite tales on this subject comes from the annals of Steve Brill. Back in 1986, the Brill-ster reportedly *bit* money-manager and future online guru James Cramer on the hand during a game of water polo. The incident was reported in the *Wall Street Journal*. Brill fired back with a phone call and lengthy memo setting the record straight from his point of view. No excuses. No apologies. Just clarification, see? Notwithstanding, the *Journal* stood by its story, possibly because Cramer was willing to testify to its veracity. He did have one correction, though: "It wasn't my hand, it was more my arm, really," he said.

Sometimes even the best miss their target.

We see similar levels of self-comfort with true princes down through the ages, from Pharaoh, who had a good reason for everything he did right up to the point where he marched his men into the Red

Sea, to Michael Milken, who behaved like a crook in order to democratize the economy.

Our most instructive Machiavelli in recent days is not Mr. Trump, nor Mr. Brill, both of whom pale in the auto-congratulations department next to perhaps the number-one performer in the history of American capitalism, "Chain Saw" Al Dunlap, the bloodiest CEO ever, who still feels great about himself, even though he is possibly the only one who does.

Until you can muster this level of self-justification, you will remain the subservient stooge you are.

During his series of eventful chairmanships at failing businesses around the nation, Mr. Dunlap was responsible for the dis-employment of tens of thousands. But he doesn't feel bad. Why should he? He was simply doing what was necessary. It's everyone else who has their head up their ass.

In his prime, Dunlap was the leading restructuring dude in the business. Under assault later, he declared that the word "restructuring"—itself a terrific euphemism—was "the most misunderstood word in our language today. People would have you translate that to mean firing people and making a lot of money. That is rubbish. Had the word been properly defined from the onset as 'rescuing,' it would not have the bad connotations."

Absolutely. Renaming a thing always makes it better.

Here are some of the things "Chain Saw" Al did. Look at them, then consider your own piddling record to date, and how far you have to go.

- At Lily Tulip, one of Al's first big corporate assignments, he cut 50 percent of the corporate staff and 20 percent of all employees. Of this approach to growth he said later, "You've got to get the right management—and that doesn't mean tweaking it a little here or a little there. . . . The people who have created the problem are not all of a sudden going to improve, so I get rid of almost all the senior management and bring in people who have worked with me before." In Chile, they called these teams of roving professionals death squads. General Pinochet hasn't apologized yet either, by the way.
- At Crown-Zellerbach, he laid off 20 percent of employees and mashed a bunch of tasty concessions out of the labor unions.
- At Consolidated Press Holdings, he sold off non-core businesses and revoked all kinds of lifestyle niceties, leaving the business leaner, and, of course, meaner.
- At Scott Paper, he laid off about one out of every three workers, about 11,000 people.
- At Sunbeam, he de-cruited more than 6,000 working men and women in very short order, driving

113

the stock price up to $54. (Wall Street loves lay-offs.) He then operated the company completely into a ditch, monkeying with the way sales were booked in order to jack up the numbers and stripping operations so badly that the wheels fell off the train. Shortly thereafter, Sunbeam stock fell to sixteen bucks.

- ⊕ Took a $35 million payoff in order to leave Sunbeam.
- ⊕ As he was cutting this swath, he had time to pen *Mean Business*, an anthem of the decade, a bestseller touted by critics and senior managers worldwide. Offered autographed copies to hotel bellhops, waiters, and, best of all, soon-to-be-laid-off workers in his employ.

This all garnered enormous praise and amused affection from Wall Street, which viewed him as a true original and rewarded him with glowing write-ups and positive analysis for decades. The business press, like *Business Week*, *Forbes*, and the *Wall Street Journal*, adored him, too, and held him up as an example of excellent management—as well they should!

The only time they asked for an apology was when the cash-flow numbers at Sunbeam started to tank. And then they fell on him like a pack of piranhas.

The end of this great Machiavellian figure came relatively swiftly and was engineered by one of his

own creations—his Sunbeam board. When they joined that august group, Dunlap demanded that they purchase Sunbeam stock *with their own money*. Ouch. He wanted them to "think like an owner." As the company moved beyond the need to slash people, performance fell. The board, which presumably was fine with everything as long as the stock was at $50, was distressed, to say the least. "You bet I looked at the company as an owner," said one member, and joined with the rest of the board to whack Al and send him home. They were mean about giving him his hard-earned $35 million severance, too, the bastards, although he did get it in the end.

"It's a lot of fun to go duck hunting, I guess," Al later told the *Houston Chronicle*. "But once the ducks start shooting back, I don't think it's fun anymore."

As with many great men, his departure was unmourned, even by members of his family. "He got exactly what he deserved," said his sister Denise.

And still he did not apologize. Not even for screwing up. Instead, not long after his departure, he took the advice of one of the most expensive public relations agencies in the United States, if not the world, and sat for an interview with the *Wall Street Journal*. Why? *Because he needed to justify himself.* He cried, too. The toughest, meanest prick in commerce shed actual tears, and worked like a dog to make sure people understood:

- He wasn't sorry;
- People got him wrong—he was a builder, not a destroyer;
- He wouldn't change a thing;
- He would be back.

And you know what? He will, too. Old Machiavellis never die. They don't fade away, either. They regenerate.

He would have no conscience to speak of

Even now, and you can look at me:
Am I a savage person? My conscience is clear.

—POL POT

The eradication of conscience is one of the toughest things you're going to have to learn. Not everyone can do it.

A conscience is an integral part of most of our makeups. We're born with it someplace inside. It's very small then, when we're little, because at that point we believe our personal needs transcend our responsibility to others, to God, to whatever. Only later does that sense of something larger than ourselves kick in.

The real Machiavellian, like the infant, believes there is nothing bigger or more important than him or herself. To succeed, you will need to achieve that view, to return to the liberating egocentrism of the selfish, amoral child who wants what he wants and permits nothing to get in its way.

Anything baby does is right, because, to a baby, self-satisfaction is the one and only value in the universe.

You, too, can eliminate your conscience by finding the inner infant within you and hauling it into the daylight. As you grow younger and younger, you will feel the part of you that punishes yourself for bad behavior disappearing. Man, does that feel good! And how free you will be to do . . . anything, really.

Back in the 1980s, for instance, Ted Turner tried to acquire CBS. He did not succeed, but his attempt crippled the company and made the ascension of Lawrence Tisch inevitable. Turner Broadcasting made $3 million in the aborted attempt, but paid $23 million in fees to lawyers and investment bankers. To this day, however, Mr. Turner reportedly feels that the failed deal was a big success, because the financial steps CBS had to undertake to fight off the unwelcome attempt placed a tremendous burden on the company, and because CBS management had to waste a lot of time deciding how to react. "We set them back ten years," was Turner's comment. He didn't seem to be too unhappy about it. Who can blame him? He's unbothered by his conscience, at least on this question, and only pissed off that he didn't get his way.

If you're a little less evolved, you will have to adjust your personality to remove as much conscience as is possible.

From this . . .

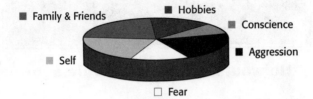

to this . . .

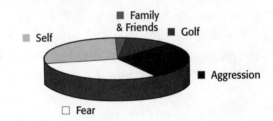

PERSONALITY COMPONENTS

You will note: The goal, in the end, is to boil yourself down to just four big essentials: aggression, fear, self—the biggest portion—and a few pals you can play golf with.

You can do it. I have confidence in you.

What Would Machiavelli Do?
✗ ✗ ✗

He would scream at people a lot

*So we're in the Ritz hotel in Paris . . . we're
disagreeing over the numbers. Suddenly Jagger
explodes: "You fat fucking record executives!"
he screams. "What do you know?" He jumps up.
I jump up. "Fuck you!" I scream back.
I'm pretty sure I can take him, but I don't want
to get into a real fistfight. He backs down. . . .
Nobody out-geschreis me.*

—WALTER YETNIKOV,
FORMER HEAD OF CBS RECORDS

*I've yelled at people, and I'm not ashamed of it. We
have to run this company efficiently and without a
bunch of babies who say, "Mommy yelled at me
today." It's impossible to run a leveraged operation
like camp. If you don't like it, leave.*

—LINDA WACHNER

It's hard to prescribe this one, but all evidence seems
to indicate that it is what Machiavelli would do. And
so we must.

I've met a few princes who did it without yelling. But they are so few . . . and they really didn't do as well, in the end, as the guys who yelled.

So it looks like, if you really want to succeed as dramatically as I know you do, you'd better start yelling at people.

Dick Snyder of Simon & Schuster was a world-famous yeller. "His profane harangues were publishing-industry legend," wrote the *Wall Street Journal*. "Scores of former employees tell of meetings where he would threaten to lop off someone's hands or private parts, or tear out their throat for some failure to perform."

Sure, it easy to criticize old yeller. But you know . . . sometimes people don't do things right. And then? Well, they have to hear about it, don't they?

Start small, with your secretary and lower-level life forms that can't strike back. You don't have to yell a lot at first, just when you really feel like it. After a while, you will begin to generate the need to yell spontaneously, about things that you used to manage without yelling. A package doesn't arrive. You really needed it. A year ago, you would have pounded around silently, gone out for a walk, counted to 110.

Now that you're doing what Machiavelli would do, however, just take the moment when you learn the package will not be arriving today, seize that feeling, and inflict it on the first couple of people you see. Try getting really loud on the very first try. See *volume* as

a barrier you have to break. Once you get used to smashing through that wall, you'll be yelling like a champ at the slightest opportunity.

From such beginnings, you will move on to yelling at people in open meetings, yelling on phones, particularly cellular phones (which can cut out at wonderful, totally sadistic moments), in elevators. . . .

If you're determined and talented, you might even graduate into a master yeller, capable of making a grown executive well into six figures blubber.

It doesn't feel good when you do it. You will always want to apologize afterward, at least in the beginning, while the vestigial skin from your human shape is still shedding. But after a while, you'll get into it.

The truth is this: A good yell is one of the finest things in executive life. It's a real release. In short, it's a rush.

So be a lioness, or a lion. Roar when you must.

It's a good thing.

122

He would establish and maintain a psychotic level of control

Every detail is important. Where do you have a meeting? What is the surrounding environment? People who don't think about these things have a harder time in business. It's got to be the right place. It's got to be the right color. It's got to be the right choice. Everything has to be strategized. You have to know where you're going to come out before you go in. Otherwise, you lose.

—MICHAEL OVITZ

Life is too complicated not to be orderly.

—MARTHA STEWART

No control, no fun. That's the rule.

You can't have a little bit of control, any more than you can be a little bit pregnant, or a little bit smart. You are a prince. You either have control, or you don't.

"Martha is as focused as a bullet in flight," said one

friend of the awesome Ms. Stewart. Anyone who has visited her perfect house in rural Connecticut sees evidence of this trait everywhere. It is flawless. The chickens, perfectly maintained in their odor-free coops, are beautiful, a myriad of breeds (if that is the right word

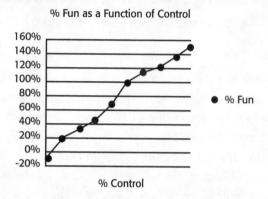

% Fun as a Function of Control

for chickens) living together in cleanliness and harmony. The kitchen, as you would expect, emits fabulous smells, even though the event may be catered. The drinks are cold and highly unusual, but not fussy. Something green, with cactus. Very strong. The grounds are manicured, naturally, but not without a certain wildness. Everything is thought out and successfully executed. When you are there, you are compelled to behave as if you belonged there. You become, as much as your imperfect nature allows you, a Martha Stewart person.

Madonna works her control lever in a different

way. "I love my meetings with suits," she says. "I *live* for meetings with suits. I love them because I know they had a really boring week and I walk in there with my orange velvet leggings and drop popcorn in my cleavage and then fish it out and eat it. I like that."

So controlling other people doesn't have to be unpleasant, for them or for you.

But it can be. Enter the unpleasant Mr. Brill.

According to *U.S. News & World Report*, there was once a young reporter by the name of Ted Rose who handed in a story to Brill, his editor. Brill immediately ripped it in half and returned it with the following note: "Ted, Have the courtesy to read your employee manual and then I will read this." It seems Rose had referred to the president as "Clinton," instead of "President Bill Clinton," a violation of the publication's style manual. "He may say, 'This guy's an asshole,' " Brill told reporter Lynn Rosellini. "But it will stick in his mind."

You know it did.

If you are not naturally a control person, life as a prince will be much more difficult for you. But there is hope. Not all control people are Control people. You don't have to have a desk you could bounce a quarter on and drawers so clean you could eat off them. You don't have to be anal to be an asshole.

Forget control over the things that almost no one

can control—the weather, your government, the stock market, traffic.

Control the things you can. Incoming phone calls. Paper. Your meeting schedule.

But most of all, control every person who is likely to cross your path and remain in it for more than five minutes. Your bosses. Your subordinates. Your office services people, who take care of your furniture. Your car service. Your friends. Your spouse. The waiters at your favorite restaurant, who you see every couple of days. The guy who regularly shines your shoes.

Forget about the world. It's big and complicated.

Control other people. Leave the rest to God.

He would follow the money, honey

*I do not like charity cases. I believe my
operations should have the sense of security that
comes from knowing their work leads to a profit.*
—SI NEWHOUSE

*The chief business of the
American people is business.*
—CALVIN COOLIDGE

While living a lavish personal life, the true prince
must be obsessively focused on the nickels and dimes
that turn into billions of dollars after a couple of quar-
terly reports.

The guy who spends 250 days a year on a company plane that costs the corporation as much as a
new building will be the first to ask whether you used
both sides of the paper.

Several years ago, while he was in the business of
wrecking CBS, teeny Lawrence Tisch was required to
have some headshots taken. This is not an unusual
occurrence in the corporate world. The executive

comes in, sits for a half hour or so, and the photographer shoots several rolls of film, the more the better, since out of three hundred shots of the average senior officer, perhaps two will be just barely usable.

On the day in question, Tisch was in the middle of several other pieces of business, lost interest immediately, and called the shoot off after three or four shots had been taken. Click, click, click—it was over before the photographer had time to warm up his electronic flash. "That's enough," said the pint-sized potentate and exited the room. Several minutes later, the photographer of the session found himself in the elevator, riding down with Tisch, who was on his way out of the building. "What happens to the rest of the film?" said Tisch to the photographer.

"I beg your pardon, sir?" said the shooter.

"How many exposures are on that film?" Tisch asked.

"Thirty-six," said the photographer, whose jaw was beginning to drop in disbelief as he realized where this was heading.

"So we only took, what, five, six shots?" said Tisch. "Don't take the film out of the camera until you use up the rest of the roll."

The doors to the elevator opened, and the CEO of the $8-billion corporation buzzed off to his next ridiculous divestiture.

This is far from unusual.

According to the *Atlanta Constitution*, in sorting his early mail one day, quintessential big-bucks entrepreneur Ted Turner noticed that every twentieth letter had a stamp without a postmark. "Hey, I said, here's a chance to make some revenue," Turner recalled. "I took the letters to our mail room and made them cut off and reuse the stamps. I figured I made a dime on every stamp." How much revenue do you think Turner's enterprises brings in every year? Answer: Enough to make such behavior pretty startling.

But that's what Machiavelli would do.

Princes who fail to sweat even the tiniest numbers tend to pay for it later. "Do I sit there and look at the bottom line all day? No," designer Donna Karan told the *Wall Street Journal* back in 1996, when her business was humming and all was well, adding in a jocular vein, "We creative types like to spend!" A year later, the *Journal* wrote:

"When Ms. Karan took her company public over a year ago, analysts and investors were invited to corporate headquarters and charmed with two glitzy evenings of wine and runway shows with Donna. Few bothered to ask a crucial question: Could a glamorous, creative designer tackle unglamorous operational tasks, like budgets, staff levels, and efficient manufacturing—not to mention the bottom line? The answer turned out to be no."

It isn't the lavish lifestyle that runs into problems with Wall Street. It's failure.

Martin Frankel, the most flamboyant and entertaining white-collar criminal in a generation, once had his limo sawed in half and extended by four inches, so his knees wouldn't touch the seat in front of him. That's living. But he also took care to make sure he had hundreds of millions of dollars illegally coming in to cover those kinds of niceties.

And while they may spring for big, fabulous expenditures when they feel like it, true princes keep their eyes on the teeny little stuff that makes them look stupid to other people.

They can't help it. They're driven, gripped by their obsessions, contemptuous of logic and consistency.

You, on the other hand, remain scrupulously consistent, meticulously logical.

When are you going to stop that?

What Would Machiavelli Do?

✗ ✗ ✗

He wouldn't be afraid to sling that bullshit

We are the most democratic country in the region.
—SLOBADAN MILOSEVIC

There is no one in New York City more loved and respected than John Gotti—loved and respected because of his hatred of drugs, scoundrels, and liars.
—BRUCE CUTLER,
JOHN GOTTI'S LEGAL ADVISOR

Give them the old Trump bullshit. Tell them it's going to be a million square feet, sixty-eight stories.
—DONALD TRUMP, TO HIS ARCHITECT

In a world of bullshitters, Donald Trump stands above all like a colossus.

"Donald is a big believer in the big-lie theory," one of his lawyers told *Vanity Fair* back in 1990. "If you say something again and again people will believe you."

This may be a bit unkind. There's no law against giving the world your construct of reality. That's just one of the things you need to do to make it come true.

What is bullshit? Research shows that the average pound of the stuff is constituted thus:

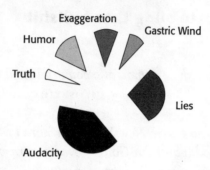

Bullshit is to be distinguished from horseshit, which is a lot smellier and has a mean and unpleasant edge to it.

Bullshit doesn't have too bad an odor, and it's easy to wash off. The minute people see it, they know what it is, and respond appropriately—"That's bullshit!" they will say, or sometimes "What a load of bullshit!" And invariably, they're right.

The ability to sling it is a gift. Some people are born to it. Others have to work to obtain it.

To Mr. Trump, it comes naturally. Back at the beginning of his real estate career in New York, he tried to buy a big piece of property being unloaded on West

Thirty-fourth Street by the Penn Central Railroad, which was in the painful process of going belly up. According to *Vanity Fair* "Trump submitted a plan for a convention center to city officials. Former deputy mayor Peter Solomon recalls: 'He told us he'd forgo his $4.4 million fee if we would name the new convention center after his father. Someone finally read the contract. He wasn't entitled to anywhere near the money he was claiming. He almost got us to name the convention center after his father in return for something he never really had to give away.'"

Well, you can't blame a fellow for trying.

Bullshitting is different than lying, however. You will note that in the above anecdote, Mr. Trump simply tried to pull a fast one on the city, hoping that they just wouldn't do their job well enough, and that he would be the beneficiary of their inattentiveness. It was Señor Trump's bad luck, on this occasion, that somebody failed to fall asleep at the switch. More often than not, however, the bullshitter will come out with more than he had any right to expect, just as a reward for his get up and go.

In this particular craft (you can't really call it an art), those who succeed must recognize *the moment of bullshit*—the instant where the choice is made not to offer a rational explanation or a thoughtful, honest response, but to sling a load in the face of the problem instead.

The verb—*to sling*—is key. The image in your mind should be of throwing a load of wet material against a barn door and seeing if any of it sticks. You do not offer bullshit. You do not put it forth. You sling it. On very rare occasions, you may, if the audience is very special, *serve it up*. But that would be the exception, not the rule. Keep in mind that slinging, as an action, requires a loose arm and a relaxed attitude. Nobody can sling while uptight or too concerned with the speed or aim of the bullshit. It's a careless action, and should be fun for both you and the recipient, although probably more fun for you if they're not expecting it and are forced to receive it with their guard down.

I assume you all are relatively practiced in the production phase of this effort. Here are some tips on delivery:

1. Sling it out there: The original impulse on Trump's part was to regale the city with a fabulous proposal that worked to his personal benefit. He launched it freely, generously, with hope in his heart and a desire to see if it would float, as he always does.

2. See if it flies: Mr. Milosevic's quote at the top of this chapter is a good example of bullshit that flew quite nicely in the arena in which it was slung, that is, greater Serbia. Just because it fell to earth outside its intended audience doesn't mean it

wasn't good bullshit. It was. Bullshit doesn't have to fly far to be good. It just has to land where you sling it.

3. Be surprised: You should always be somewhat shocked when your bullshit is discovered. "Wow," you should say, "is that mine?" Then you can find out what other folks are making of your bullshit and respond accordingly. If necessary, you can toss a little extra after it, because . . .

4. There's more where that came from: The only antidote to a bullshit situation is more bullshit. Never attempt to rectify bullshit gone bad with anything other than more bullshit, unless you want to change the game entirely.

5. Laugh, clown, laugh! You gotta laugh. It's just bullshit, isn't it?

There is a time, however, when bullshit should cease and you should once again reenter the world of truth and lies. President Clinton, for example, would have done well to stop bullshitting the American people when it was clear we were on to the depth and quality of his material. This would have disarmed his adversaries, who were even then quite successfully fighting his load with theirs.

A good load of truth (or a direct lie) always and immediately neutralizes even the most powerful bullshit and ups the ante into the real, non-bullshit world,

if such a place exists. Keep that in mind when you're loading up for your next opportunity.

And don't get caught too often. Having a reputation as a prime bullshitter only works for some professionals—public relations people, real estate agents, investment bankers in search of a transaction fee, security analysts who work for brokerages. Genuine bankers, physicians, the occasional journalist, and other individuals who make their money earning the public trust should be careful where they sling it, and of how easy it will be to quietly get it back if the time comes to deny having thrown it.

You don't want to hear the chairman of the Fed chuckling merrily and exclaiming, "Hey, guys! Did I say that?"

What Would Machiavelli Do?
✗ ✗ ✗

He would eat to kill

For the new entrepreneur,
it's eat lunch or be lunch, really.
—SCOTT MCNEALY, CEO, SUN MICROSYSTEMS

Mao Tse-Tung said it best: An army marches on its stomach. I don't think he meant it literally, since it's impossible to actually walk on your stomach for any protracted period of time, even in China, which is on the other side of the world and does things very differently.

But you know, I think Mao was talking about something else.

Food is more than sustenance. It is who you are, as a warrior. It is perhaps the greatest weapon in your fight to conquer others. As a tool for friendship, too, it cannot be beat.

But you can't get where you want to be by eating nice. As mean as you are in all other things, you must also *eat mean*. Lucretia Borgia, who was Italian, I think, and may have actually lived at the time of Machiavelli, routinely poisoned her adversaries. She

had rings made up with hidden compartments beneath large jewels. At a perfectly nice drinks session, she would lean over and dump a load of mercury into your wine, and that was that for you.

You can't actually use poison. But there are plenty of foods that can ruin other people for business. Then you can swoop down on them.

Let's start at the top of the day.

Breakfast. The most important meal for hurting other people. Bacon is your most effective tool. Get the other person to eat a lot of it. It's fatty and salty and delicious, and they will get slow and childish as they eat it, and start feeling self-indulgent and happy. You can find out a lot about them in this state.

Listen to men, in particular, after they have been convinced to have a big, eggy breakfast. This is a good time to get raises or changes in your contract, or plant noxious gossip in a receptive ear. Lay a guy out with a big breakfast before your next negotiating session. Watch his eyes droop at around eleven o'clock. Then go for it.

Brunch. Laze around reading newspapers at the beach. Talk about news. Look! Waffles! Talk about that issue you wanted to resolve. What can go wrong? Work hard to overdose the other guy on coffee—and maybe even booze!—hyping him or her up to feverish

pitch in which you can exploit his deranged mind to your benefit.

Lunch. Lunch, for the most part, should be reserved primarily for yourself and a few friends who are willing to sit with you without bothering you too much. It's hard to make a sober lunch into a blunt instrument.

Absent that, you could try to get the other guy to eat something excessively virtuous that he or she does not like. This will leave them disappointed and more vulnerable in the later part of the meal. Foods that are not conducive to your destabilization effort include: peanut butter and jelly, chicken fingers, fish sticks, hot dogs (while seated), and, for older executives, mashed potatoes with gravy, all of which provide the kind of primal sustenance that helps people perform better in your face.

Booze. Face it: Drink is poison. This in itself is not a bad thing. Poisons are very useful tools. Self-poisoning is always a danger, however, so you have to be careful.

There is a boneheaded notion about that business cannot be conducted when people have been drinking. This is nonsense. Henry the Eighth nearly destroyed Catholicism in England during a time period when the water was so bad that people drank two or three gallons of strong ale per day instead. Winston Churchill

was a complete rummy. No, that's unfair. Brandy was his drink, and he began the day with it, like mouth-wash, chased by the first of many enormous cigars.

Drink beer or wine, unless you are Winston Churchill, or you have a lifetime of experience abusing liquor and are still marginally not an alcoholic. If you get stupid on hard liquor, do not drink hard liquor. I have seen in my time men and women who could not handle their liquor provide much, much amusement. God bless them, wherever they are.

Your goal is, while drinking yourself, to establish and maintain an *increasingly superior level of sobriety* than the person across the table from you. Depending on what you need to do, you can manipulate the drunk or put him completely on his ass.

Dinner. This is where the real hitters come out to sign, seal, and deliver the future. Breakfast, face it, is for bullshitters. That's not a knock on the institution or its practitioners, where would we be without them? Lunch is fine, but people have to go back to work. Just when you're ready for the kill, they get to escape. It's very frustrating. Dinner is where the game is played for keeps. Some suggestions:

⊕ Don't go into a dinner without a clear idea of what you want out of it. Otherwise, you could get played, instead of the other way around.

- If you're doing business with moguls, eat meat— as rare as you can stand it. Impress the other guy with how big and red your meat is.
- If you must eat fish, make sure it's a huge piece. And rare. Very, very rare.
- Never eat any foodstuff that was invented after 1990. What is monkfish? Did you ever see any before you were an adult? Don't you think that's kind of weird? And don't eat kiwi. It's over.
- Always pick up the check. A little baby with a diaper and a bib has his food provided for him. A prince pays his own way.

Nightcaps. Necessary if you're planning to sleep with your companion. Otherwise, I don't get the concept. You were drunk enough several hours ago. Unless you're going to sign a deal right there or take your companion up to his or her room for a shag, maybe it's time to go home, baby.

Finally, a word about midnight snacks: Do not believe, because everyone else is in the arms of Morpheus and nothing much is going on that this is not a potential business situation for the true Machiavellian. Au contraire. It's cool, and silent, and dark, and if you sit there with that steak bone both you and the dog have had your eye on since Sunday, who knows? You just might get that idea you've been looking for. Sleep is overrated anyway.

What Would Machiavelli Do?
✗ ✗ ✗

He would never retire

Did you hear the one about the guy
who walks into the shrink's office with
the duck on his head?

— FORMER BOSS WHO RETIRED AT FIFTY

Have you ever been to Florida? Not Disneyworld, where it's 110 degrees in the shade and people are enjoying themselves to death, basically. Not Miami, where beautiful people gather down by the Clevelander Hotel to play with their pet iguanas. I'm talking about the Florida where people go to relax, play golf, and die. You don't want to go there. Not ever. Plan on keeling over one afternoon while sitting at your desk and yelling at somebody instead. You'll be glad you did.

People who retire have the whole thing planned out in advance. They think they will have a good time doing a wide variety of zesty things. And for the first couple of years, that probably happens. After that, though, the pleasure curve on most retirement activities goes something like this:

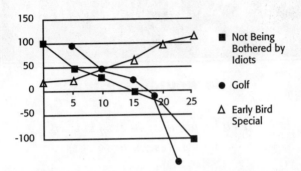

You will note that the interest in golf and not being bothered by idiots fades over time, as skills get dulled with age and the novelty of doing the same thing every day wears thin. Appreciation for premature meals, however, seems to rise until all one is doing during retirement is eating several hours before people who work for a living. This is a relatively limited palette for enjoyment.

Every now and then I bump into an old boss of mine. He retired very young and is very rich. We hug when we see each other, and he asks me what is going on, and I tell him, and he looks a little wistful, and then I ask him what's going on, and he tells me about how he just got back from Spain, where he spent time with Seve Ballesteros. And I look in his eyes, and there is nothing there.

He seems happy, though.

He would have fun

It's a beautiful day. Let's play two.
— ERNIE BANKS, CHICAGO CUBS

Remember two things, as we part:

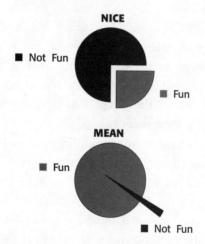

NICE

■ Not Fun

■ Fun

MEAN

■ Fun

■ Not Fun

Which is better?
Don't forget it.
Good luck and good hunting, my prince.

WHAT WOULD MACHIAVELLI *NOT* DO?

He would not be a jerk.

A couple of months ago, the New York tabloids were full of front-page stories of unbearable piquancy for the residents of this jaded town. The papers were gleefully hollering in thousand-point type about a decision made by the greatest over-Machiavellian of our age: New York City Mayor Rudolph Giuliani.

Hizzoner had done it again. He was faced with the possibility that Tina Brown's new *Talk* magazine would kick off its debut issue with a party celebrating its first cover subject—his potential opponent for the Senate, Hillary Rodham Clinton. Engorged with rage, the mayor canceled the organizers' permit to hold their bash at the Brooklyn Navy Yard.

"Party Pooper!" screamed the *New York Daily News*. Opinion on the street and around the water coolers was much the same. Once again, the mayor, who had done such a good job in so many things, was showing the leather truncheoned, jack-booted side of his personality. He was canceling the party . . . because he could.

He had acted in similar fashion before. One week, for instance, he decided to reroute all the foot traffic in midtown, and assigned dozens of police officers to make sure pedestrians crossed the street where he wanted them to. No real attempt was made to communicate why this was being done. It was just better for us, and so we were expected to do it. Traffic was improved, we were told. It didn't feel improved, but what if it was? People were disgusted anyway. We're New Yorkers! Shouldn't we be able to cross Fifth Avenue wherever the hell we want? Apparently not.

Every day, the mayor is kicking somebody's ass.

By spring 1999, a *Daily News* poll found that more citizens of New York City—at least that week—favored Hillary Clinton as a Senate candidate than were for Giuliani, a mayor they generally saw as doing a good job in a very tough role. In other words, a lot of people despised the mayor in spite of the fact that they thought he was terrific.

Moderation, it turns out, is always called for, even in the use of power. It is possible for very big players

to out-Machiavelli Machiavelli himself. But it doesn't help them any.

Consider Kenneth Starr, long after his pursuit of the president ended in what has to be considered some kind of victory—even for a malicious, desiccated fellow like him—chasing low-level functionaries who played golf with somebody who might have heard that the president's wife did indeed fire those people in the White House Travel Office. Bah.

Consider Bill Gates, obsessively reaching out to crush any web browsing system that he could not own or control with such ferocity that he left an uncharacteristically stupid paper trail in the ultimate headquarters of the paperless universe. Pfui.

Consider Bill Clinton, cleverly molding and sculpting a variety of English verbs, when a simple "Hey, folks, I'm a baaad dog" would have sufficed.

Or Richard Nixon with his brilliant idea to tape conversations in the Oval Office. Or George III deciding to teach those rude colonials a serious lesson. Pilate washing his hands, and thinking the whole sloppy mess was behind him. Pharaoh snubbing Moses. Satan disrespecting God. Every single one got what was coming to him, eventually. In a very big way.

Good may often be its own—and only—reward in this competitive, malevolent, and unfair world. This may be most true in business, where the unsympa-

thetic aspects of human character are compensated most lavishly. But evil does have its limitations, ones that even the biggest, baddest Machiavellis around should keep in mind.

That may be the very best—and most useful— lesson of all.